COMING HOME

COMING HOME

Why Protestant Clergy Are Becoming Orthodox

Edited by Peter E. Gillquist

Ancient Faith Publishing
Chesterton, Indiana

COMING HOME:
Why Protestant Clergy Are Becoming Orthodox
© Copyright 1992, Peter E. Gillquist

Second edition, 1995

Published by
    Ancient Faith Publishing
    (A division of Ancient Faith Ministries)
    P.O. Box 748
    Chesterton, IN 46304

ISBN: 978-0-9622713-2-8

Library of Congress Cataloguing in Publication Data

Coming home: why Protestant clergy are becoming Orthodox/
    edited by Peter E. Gillquist.
                p. cm.
    ISBN 0-9622713-2-2
    1. Converts, Orthodox Eastern--Biography.
    2. Protestant churches--Clergy--Biography.
    I. Gillquist, Peter E.
    BX390.C65   1992
    281.9'092'2'--dc20
    [B]   92-23727
                                                 CIP

*The kingdom of heaven is like a
merchant seeking beautiful pearls, who,
when he had found one pearl of great price,
went and sold all that he had and bought it.*
—Matthew 13:45,46

CONTENTS

Preface .... Page 11

Chapter One:
    Orthodox Revival at ORU .... Page 15
Chapter Two:
    From Evangelical to Orthodox .... Page 23
Chapter Three:
    Forbidden Gates and Royal Doors.................... Page 35
Chapter Four:
    The Last Train Home....................................... Page 45
Chapter Five:
    It Happened at Western Conservative .... Page 53
Chapter Six:
    A Convert from Within.................................... Page 61
Chapter Seven:
    Asbury Dreams and Orthodox Realities .... Page 67
Chapter Eight:
    The Pearl of Great Price .... Page 75
Chapter Nine:
    After Forty Years .... Page 81
Chapter Ten:
    Back to Pentecost.. Page 89
Chapter Eleven:
    Who Says the Bible Says? .... Page 95

Chapter Twelve:
    Where Foundations Will Not Change ....Page 103
Chapter Thirteen:
    Our Surprising Salvation ....Page 111
Chapter Fourteen:
    Sent Away to the Ancient Faith ....Page 119
Chapter Fifteen:
    Orthodoxy Comes to Wheaton ....Page 127
Chapter Sixteen:
    From Biola to the Barrio ....Page 135
Chapter Seventeen:
    In the Breaking of the Bread ....Page 141
Chapter Eighteen:
    An Anglican–Orthodox Pilgrimage..................Page 151

PREFACE

Why are Protestant Pastors
Becoming Orthodox?

The idea for this book began at an editorial meeting for AGAIN Magazine, the quarterly publication of the Antiochian Evangelical Orthodox Mission. Our editor, Father Weldon Hardenbrook, our managing editor, Deacon Ray Zell, and I were brainstorming ideas for future issues. In the course of our conversation we realized each of us had been receiving a large and growing number of phone calls and letters from Protestant pastors interested in finding out more about the Orthodox Faith.

"Is this a growing trend," we asked ourselves, "and if so, what's behind it?"

A Special Issue

We decided to plan a special issue of AGAIN asking a representative group of Protestant pastors who have recently become Orthodox to tell us why they came, and to answer the question "Why Are Protestant Schools Producing Orthodox Clergy?"

As the responses began coming in, we realized how significant this topic might be for our readers. The accounts were inspiring, educational, sometimes amusing, and often heart-rending. To hear from so many different men—all dedicated pastors and Church leaders who served with dedication in their various denominations, and to hear how God worked to bring them to the ancient Orthodox Faith—was one of the most uplifting projects any of us had worked on. At times it resembled Pentecost, as people from incredibly diverse backgrounds came together to unite within the walls of the Church established on that day.

The Response

No sooner did AGAIN hit the mailboxes than letters from our readers began coming in. This was the most popular issue of AGAIN Magazine ever produced! We heard from readers all over the country, and from overseas, who like us were greatly inspired and encouraged by these stories. Within a matter of weeks, we had received enough requests for extra copies and bulk orders to deplete our entire supply of back issues.

Rather than reprint the issue by itself, we decided to publish a book of these accounts. We would add to this collection similar stories we had run in the past, and solicit a number of new chapters. Although we broadened our perspective slightly, including more than just stories of college and seminary grads who had become priests, the basic scope and intent of the book remains unchanged.

What can we say about the current crop of Protestant leaders now coming to Orthodoxy?

First, numerous Protestant clergy and lay people alike are becoming aware of the Orthodox Faith for the first time. The fear often exists that because of ethnic differences which undeniably exist between East and West, Orthodoxy Christianity will swallow them up into a cultural identity with which they cannot relate. Others see Orthodoxy as highly intriguing and even tempting, but too difficult to learn. Who better than recent converts to speak to these concerns?

Second, there are lifelong Orthodox Christians who need to catch a fresh vision of the priceless treasure which is theirs in this historic Faith. Often, newcomers to the Church can impart that vision better than anyone else.

Third, for those motivated by a desire for better understanding across confessional lines, those writing in this book are commendably candid as to the reasons they changed. Personally, I was moved by these journeys of fellow pastors who hold a deep and abiding love for Christ and His Kingdom.

Gratitude

You will notice something else in these stories: not one speaks flippantly concerning either the schools or the denominational backgrounds out of which they came. We were not looking for ecclesiastical malcontents to contribute. These pastors see their calling as coming from God. They are thankful for the good things their traditions had to offer. It was because of, not in spite of, their heritage that they have found their way to the fullness of the Orthodox Faith.

Are we on the front end of a discovery of and a movement toward Orthodox Christianity here in North America? Or do we have here but a brief rolling of the drums which will be heard for a time, then fall silent? Perhaps it is too soon to tell, but the stories herein could certainly hold clues to the answers to these questions.

In this regard I am impressed with one last thing. Almost every author shares his fervent desire for the New Testament

Church, the Faith of the Apostles, the Pearl of Great Price, authentic worship in spirit and in truth—in short, original Christianity. And that is precisely what true Orthodox life has to offer.

Fr. Peter E. Gillquist
Publisher, AGAIN Magazine

Chapter One

ORTHODOX REVIVAL AT ORU

By Fr. Antony Hughes

Whathat a strange turn of events! Conversions at Oral Roberts University were not unusual, certainly. People were "born again" there all the time. But conversions to Holy Orthodoxy? Not what you would expect in a major charismatic center.

Nevertheless, in the late seventies and early eighties a small, but significant, number of students discovered the Holy, Catholic, and Apostolic Church and left everything to join her! I was one of them.

Enclosed in our private world of Tulsa, Oklahoma, we converts to Orthodoxy were not aware of the "splash" our conversions would make. When I finally arrived at Saint Vladimir's Seminary for a one-year program, I was greeted by a professor from France with the words, "Oh, you are one of *them!* We heard of you in Paris!" This was at least seven years after my graduation from ORU. Needless to say, our conversions took the ORU administration, faculty, and student body by surprise. They took us by surprise as well.

Theology I

The initial contact many of us had with the Orthodox Faith came during our very first class in Systematic Theology I. The professor began the class in the usual way, with prayer, but not with a prayer we could recognize. He started off with the sign of the cross made curiously backwards! A series of invocations to the Holy Trinity, a few "Lord, have mercies," and a "Glory to the Father" brought us at last to familiar territory, the Lord's Prayer. But even that had a surprise ending.

Stranger yet was his closing prayer mentioning someone called "Theotokos." Who was this? Better yet, who was this professor, how did he get in here, and what were we to make of him? As we retook our seats hoping and praying for some explanation, our dauntless professor launched into a reading from one of the suggested text books, *The Lives of the Desert Fathers* by Helen Waddell. The selection was, no less, "The Life of Saint Pelagia the Harlot."

For our motley crew of Pentecostals, disenfranchised Protestants, evangelicals, charismatics, and wayfaring Catholics, this rich menu of Orthodox spirituality was a tremendous shock. Some students reacted with anger, while others, myself included, were intrigued if not downright moved. I purposed to search out the answers to my multitude of questions.

The pilgrimage was on! We formed a study group to accomplish two things: 1) to find a way to pass Systematic

Theology I and II, and 2) to try and digest as much as possible of this new (read: *old*) way of approaching Christianity. We did battle with heretics, studied each Ecumenical Council in depth, grappled with Church history, apostolic succession, apophatic theology, Vladimir Lossky, and, of course, the Bible.

We rediscovered the Protestant Reformation, only this time in a much broader context, that of the whole of Church history instead of just medieval Roman Catholicism. We learned a new definition of Tradition from the Orthodox perspective: "the life of the Holy Spirit in the Church."

Our vistas began to expand. There were alternatives to the Christianity we had known, and one of them was looking better and better to a growing number of students both in the seminary and in the undergraduate school.

Change-Points

For me there were several key turning points. The first was the study of Church history. Sitting in my Southern Baptist Church in Erwin, Tennessee as a youngster I never dreamed there was anything to predate it. I couldn't even name the preacher who came before Pastor Faulkner, much less the names of any saints or Church Fathers (except Billy Graham and Lottie Moon)! That the Church could be historically traced to Christ and the Apostles was a watershed. There were some in my Church who literally believed that Saint John the Baptist was the founder of the Southern Baptist convention and after him came Roger Williams. From ancient Palestine to colonial Rhode Island was quite a jump!

The second turning point was the discovery of liturgy in the early Church. I had gravitated towards the liturgical traditions since high school, but without anything other than a love for

Christian aesthetics and a growing respect for ritual to guide me. Now there were other reasons to legitimate my interest.

The third was a bombshell: the New Testament was not written by parachurch evangelists! In fact, the Church existed *before* the New Testament. It was the Church which gave birth to the Gospels and Epistles, not the other way around.

After our conversions we placed an ad for our local parish in the ORU paper which read, "Looking for a Bible-based Church? Why not the Church that gave you the Bible?" This more realistic (actually holistic) view of Holy Scripture coupled with the remarkable interpretive tradition of Orthodoxy made the Bible come alive in ways we had never dreamed possible.

These, among other things, helped to cement my own decision to convert. I have no doubt they influenced the others as well.

During the Lenten season of 1979 we learned of a retreat to be held in Wichita, Kansas. The retreat master would be none other than Father Alexander Schmemann. We organized a group to attend. To this day I cannot remember the subject, nor can I remember anything Father Schmemann said. What I do remember is that his words and the worship impressed me. But I was impressed with something else as well. The people in attendance seemed to be "tuned in" to their Church and extremely knowledgeable about their Faith, and yet they were simply "the folks in the pews."

Frankly, questioning the commitment of Orthodox Christians to Christ, "bound" as they were to liturgy and tradition, was a common practice of some in our group. What we learned is that Orthodox piety is sober, thoughtful, and distrustful of the emotionalism which made up the greatest percentage of the practice we were gradually leaving behind. But this hardly meant that Orthodox spirituality was less "personal."

The Orthodox doctrines of deification and synergy spoke of a union with God far more intense than the Protestant juridical understanding. The sacraments were not merely optional, ancient rituals; they were absolutely essential to a fully-developed incarnational Christology and to salvation. The liturgy, sacraments, Tradition, communion of the saints, the approach to spirituality itself, were part of a seamless robe whose very fabric was the Apostolic Faith. It was in Wichita that I decided to do what my heart had been telling me to do since that first day in Systematic Theology class. To be honest with myself, I knew I had to become Orthodox.

Narrowing the Choices

There is much more, of course, to the story. After a year of seminary at ORU, I joined the Episcopal Church, thinking that it might be a good place to "mark time." Not wanting to leave a stone unturned I attended three Churches: I first went to the Episcopal service at Saint Andrews at 9:00 A.M., then hurried to the Orthodox Divine Liturgy at Saint Antony's at 11:00, and then spent my Sunday evenings receiving private instruction from a kindly Benedictine priest at a local Roman parish for about five months.

I left the smorgasbord of evangelicalism and the charismatic movement behind in the dust once my mind began to turn. I knew that there were others at school moving in the same direction. Our relationships forged in the study group survived its demise. Some were moving more slowly than I could allow for myself. At last Orthodoxy came out on top in the "battle of catholic traditions" (no holds barred, unlimited rounds) and after about six months of further instruction from the pastor of Saint Antony's, the Very Reverend Michael Keiser, I was chrismated on a beautiful Palm

Sunday morning.

The presence of an English-speaking Antiochian parish with a dedicated priest and a community open to receive me was immensely important. Although I first learned of Orthodox Christianity in class and in books, I would never have seen it in the flesh without the parish. Father Michael was himself a convert, so he understood very well the dynamics of conversion and the effects it might have on his predominantly Lebanese parish. The chrismation of one might not shake things up, but I was soon to be followed by groups of others scattered throughout the coming year and a half. Father Michael's job was not always easy, but our incorporation into his parish was as graceful as could be expected.

Back at ORU

The reactions at ORU to our conversions were mixed. Some professors and students were supportive while others grew defensive. I'll never forget the response of one professor who told me angrily, "This is the worst mistake you have ever made!" Another said, "The Orthodox Church is only for those who cannot stand on their own two feet!" My mental reply to the latter was, "How true." Drs. O'Malley and Losoncy, however, stand out in my mind as two of those who responded with understanding and compassion. Others like them provided an example of Christian love that will remain in my mind for years to come.

You may wonder how Oral Roberts himself responded. I really do not know, but I did hear of a sermon he preached after I had already graduated in which he took pains to explain to the student body that all his teachings agreed with those of the Holy Fathers of the ancient Church!

The reasons for our conversions at ORU cannot be boiled

down to any kind of strategy. Clearly the shock treatment of the Systematics professor did not account for all the conversions. Some of us who joined the Orthodox Church were not present for those classes. There was no organized evangelism in any sense. This was a purely spontaneous movement directed, I believe, by the Holy Spirit.

One of my compadres, now a priest, put it this way: "The Holy Spirit found a few warm hearts in which to dwell." The fact is that the message of Orthodoxy reached only a few, but the legacy continues. Six priests have been produced from among our company. Another convert is on the faculty of Saint Tikhon's Seminary in Pennsylvania and there are still other converts coming from ORU. The library is liberally equipped with the best in Orthodox literature (the Systematics professor was also in charge of library acquisitions!) and the work of the community of Saint Antony's in Tulsa continues.

Could it happen again?

As with all true movements of the Holy Spirit, "The wind blows where it wishes, and you hear the sound of it, but cannot tell where it comes from and where it goes" (John 3:8). As such, we believe that in God's own time, and for the sake of His Church, born on the day of Pentecost, this calling back of God's people to the historic Church can and must happen again—and again, and again—in this country.

For us, this wind first arose in a college classroom in Oklahoma. Before it was finished blowing, we had become full-time priests in the Orthodox Church in North America. Where will it appear next? Perhaps in a place even *less* likely than the campus of Oral Roberts University.

Chapter Two

FROM EVANGELICAL TO ORTHODOX

By Fr. Gregory Rogers

Perhaps I have always been spiritually hungry. Growing up in a devoted Christian home, I do not remember ever *not* believing in Christ, or *not* wanting in my heart of hearts to follow Him and do His will. Not that I was always able to fulfill that desire moment by moment, but the desire was certainly there.

I did all the things that good Christian boys are supposed to do. Baptized by profession of faith shortly before my ninth birthday, I attended services, youth meetings, Sunday school, went to Church camp each summer, participated in youth rallies, service projects, read the Scriptures and nearly anything else I could get my hands on. By the time I was in junior high there was no doubt in my mind that I would enter the ministry in some way, shape, or form. I preached my first sermon (on prayer) in the ninth grade, taught Sunday School, and even taught the "Know What You Believe" series of classes at the Lake Region Christian Assembly the summer after my junior year of high school.

After graduation, I entered Lincoln Christian College in Lincoln, Illinois, to prepare myself for ministry in the Christian Churches/Churches of Christ (a conservative evangelical Protestant sect, historically rooted in the Restoration Movement begun by Alexander Campbell and others on the American frontier in the early nineteenth century). Always restless, as college students often are, and desiring to apply the things I was learning in a practical way, I took a position as Youth Minister at the Deep River Church of Christ in Merrillville, Indiana, at the tender age of 18, while still a freshman.

Perhaps the best word to describe my approach to ministry at that point was *serious*. I was not interested in building a youth program that was founded purely upon social events and gimmicks designed to draw people into the Church on a superficial level. The most important aspect of life was a relationship with Christ that touched the very center of one's being. So I worked to build a strong core of committed young people, seeking to make Jesus Lord over every aspect of life.

Going Deeper

In this period, two themes dominated much of my thinking and effort: spirituality and Church. One morning during my prayers, in all sincerity, but without a clue as to what I was really saying, I told the Lord, "More than anything else, Lord, I want to be a spiritual man. I am willing to pay any price or bear any burden to become one. I don't really know what that is or means, but that is what I want." In many respects, much of the subsequent history of my life can be seen as an answer, or at least a developing answer, to that prayer. I wanted to know God, not just know about Him. I wanted to experience the sense of His presence, to grow in faith, hope, and love. And I wanted to see His power worked in others through me, to see healing and repentance, growth and conversion in the lives of the people among whom I ministered.

My spiritual search led me in several different directions. I tried the teachings of Watchman Nee. I read C. S. Lewis, Francis Schaeffer, Dietrich Bonhoeffer, Jacques Ellul, and others. I read the works of charismatic leaders and sought to experience the reality of the Spirit of God that they seemed to touch. I worked on cultivating a life of prayer, with mixed results. I seemed to be unable to satisfy the longing that was within me for the experience of God, and powerless to overcome "the sin that so easily beset" me.

At the same time, I was struggling with the whole idea of what the Church of Jesus Christ was really called to be. The scriptural descriptions of the Church were certainly not true to what I was experiencing in my life. Saint Paul called the Church "[Christ's] body, the fullness of Him Who fills all in all" (Ephesians 1:23). Where was this fullness?

Worship in our tradition was weak at best. Our services consisted of a couple of songs, a brief communion service (conceived of as a meditative memorial on Christ's death), and a sermon. The sermons were usually good, instructive, inspiring, evangelical. But our services resembled good motivational lectures more than worship. Where was God? Where was the acknowledgment of His presence? Why were we together?

I also longed to experience community in the Church.

The body of Christ is an image of interdependence, of connectedness. In much of my Christian life I was experiencing isolation. The Church community was not caring for one another like it should. Our system of pastoral care was inadequate to look after the needs of the people of God.

Starting From Scratch

For some time I worked on reforming and developing these things in the Church where I served. But it became apparent that the kinds of things for which I was longing could never be found in the structure inherent in my situation. The expressions of worship could only go as far as the tradition of the Christian Churches would allow. And I believed God was wanting to take me on a spiritual journey like that of Abraham, to a land of which I knew not.

So, in July of 1977, my wife, Pamela, and I left our ministry and unknowingly began our pilgrimage to Orthodoxy. A few friends gathered around us and we formed a small congregation dedicated to the pilgrimage. Everything was up for grabs, save the deity of Christ and the authority of the Scriptures. We consciously decided to reexamine all our beliefs in the light of the Scriptures and the experience of God's people through the centuries. And we committed ourselves to do the best we could to put into practice what we learned.

Through the relationships we had with dear friends from our days at Lincoln Christian College, we linked ourselves to the group of Churches connected with what was then the New Covenant Apostolic Order (later the Evangelical Orthodox Church). Together with these brethren, we examined a number of specific areas which we felt were of primary significance to our developing movement. These areas included:

1) Worship. I was partial to a loose, spontaneous, charismatic kind of approach toward worship, and expected to find that in the Scriptures and in history. To our surprise, our spontaneity itself began to lead us to order in worship, everything taking on a familiar pattern. Our study of the writings of Justin Martyr (about A.D. 150) showed us that the Church has always had some kind of liturgical form to its worship. Even the New Testament showed evidences of this in the use of hymns and in the description of the meetings. So we began using liturgical forms of worship.

2) Scriptural Interpretation. Our theological studies led us to understand something that had never dawned on me before, that the Scriptures needed to be interpreted in the context of Tradition. In the Church in which I had been raised, it was fashionable to say, "No creed but Christ, no book but the Bible, no name but the Divine." Yet, on the back of every Sunday bulletin was a statement saying, "We believe. . ." and listing several items ranging from the nature of salvation, who Christ is, and what constitutes a valid Christian baptism. What else is this except a creed? In fact, our three-part slogan above is creedal! And our positions were derived within the context of a tradition—the Campbellite tradition.

We came to realize that the Bible does not exist in a vacuum or stand on its own apart from interpretation. The question was not "tradition or no tradition?", but, "which tradition?" Are we to accept theological positions that are derived only from our own limited experience, or are we to examine and give authoritative weight to the consensual teachings of the Church through her history? We began to ask ourselves, then, how are we to interpret the teachings of the Scripture, and on what basis are we to evaluate the traditions we see?

We found at least the foundation of an answer in the writings of Saint Vincent of Lerins, a Latin father of the fifth century. In his *Commonitory*, he cites three criteria for determining whether a doctrine is in keeping with the truth of the gospel. They are: a) *universality*: has this doctrine been believed everywhere in the Christian world and in every time by all, or almost all, of the recognized teachers of the Church?; b) *antiquity:* can this doctrine be found, at least in seed form, in the teachings of the Apostles, and maintained by the Fathers of the Church?; and c) *consensus:* has this doctrine been held by an ecumenical council, or by the broad consensus of the Fathers of the Church?

Using this hermeneutical structure, we began to examine doctrines and practices of both the historic and contemporary Churches. The results were revolutionary. We discovered that the Church's worship had *always* been liturgical, founded in the practices of the Jewish synagogue and temple worship. So our worship became liturgical, modeled after the same pattern used in the historic Church.

3) The Sacraments. In our reexamination of the sacraments of the Church, we discovered the Eucharist is more than just a memorial of the cross of Christ; it is a partaking in a mystery of His glorified human nature, a sharing in His body and blood, a tasting of the powers of the age to come. Rather than being an addendum to worship, it is the focal point of our worship, the moment at which we supremely commune with God and experience His presence in the deepest portion of our being.

Baptism is a sacramental means by which we are joined into union with Christ and share the likeness of His death and the power of His Resurrection. Doctrines such as the Trinity and the Incarnation were no longer obscure, but came to be central in our understanding of God and who we are in relationship to Him. Our salvation was shown to be not merely a mental assent to truth, but a living, sacramental union with Him which transforms everything that we are into His image and likeness.

4) The Church. Our studies also focused on the nature of Church itself. We began to see that an independent congregational form of government was alien both to the New Testament and to the early Church. Of all things, we began to see the Church needed leadership from all four orders: bishops, priests, deacons, and the laity. We were strongly influenced by the writings of Saint Ignatius of Antioch in devising the structure of our sphere of Churches.

Protestant Orthodox

In 1979, it became apparent we were more than a loose confederation of Churches: we were in fact a denomination with a governing structure and a common set of beliefs. So we organized the Evangelical Orthodox Church on February 15, 1979, declaring ourselves to be, so far as we understood, "A denomination within the One, Holy, Catholic, and Apostolic Church."

Our studies and pilgrimage continued over the next few years as we worked our way through the Seven Ecumenical Councils of the undivided Church, and found ourselves committed to the teachings of those councils. Realizing that our theological framework placed us in the same category of thinking as the Orthodox Church, we actively began seeking a way to enter into communion with Orthodoxy. At the same time we continued to develop theologically, coming to a fuller understanding of Mary's role in our salvation, and of the veneration of the saints and of icons.

In the fall of 1981, in an effort to draw upon the expertise of others and to learn as much as possible about the history of the Church, I entered into a program at the University of Chicago Divinity School in the History of Christianity. In 1983, I finished a master of arts in divinity degree, and at this writing have completed my qualifying exams towards my Ph.D.

During this period of time, we began to discover some of the riches of Orthodox spirituality. To this point, we were experiencing the blessing of God in our corporate worship; we began to find Him more and more in our personal worship. For years I had struggled with consistency in my prayer life, trying to have devotions morning and evening. After failing at that, I cultivated the practice of prayer throughout the day, attempting what Saint Paul called prayer without ceasing.

Orthodox spirituality showed me a way to consistently approach God, one that would enable me to pray irrespective of my mood, my creativity, my spontaneity. Orthodoxy's emphasis on a rule of prayer, a consistent set of prayers to pray regularly, set my prayer free from enslavement to myself and my spiritual prowess. Further, the Jesus Prayer became an enrichment in my effort to cultivate the presence of God throughout the day. We eagerly read the works of Orthodox spiritual writers such as Theophan the Recluse, Metropolitan Anthony Bloom, and, of course, the writings of the Fathers of the Church, particularly the *Philokalia*.

More and more, we were becoming Orthodox in our outlook, our theology, our worship, our spirituality. The major issue facing us now was our relationship to the historic

Orthodox Church. For some of us in the Evangelical Orthodox Church, it seemed enough to continue to do our best to recapture those things we saw in the ancient Church which needed to be restored in our age. In a way we were really Protestant Orthodox—Orthodox in many ways, but Protestant in our ecclesiology. Just as many Protestants believe they can look at the Scriptures, discern the proper blueprint for Church life, put that into practice, and call themselves the Church, so we thought we could recreate the practices of the One, Holy, Catholic, and Apostolic Church and by so doing we could be such.

We began to see, however, that the Church is not built by following a blueprint. The body of Christ is a living organism, one that has had a continuous sacramental life over twenty centuries. If it were really "the fullness of Him who fills all in all," it could not have died, only to be re-created and restored by us after all these years.

So the questions became not *what* is the Church, but *where* is the Church? Once we came to see that the true Church is in historic continuity with the Church of the Apostles, the undivided One, Holy, Catholic, and Apostolic Church of the first Christian millennium, we realized that we must become sacramentally integrated into the Orthodox Church. It was not enough to copy her structures, doctrines, and practices. We must be integrated into her life, to participate in her history, and to share in her heavenly life, experiencing the life of Christ in communion with her.

The Church of Jesus Christ
By the grace of God, in 1987, we presented ourselves to the Orthodox Church, not as reformers, nor as critics, but as

pilgrims who had been on a long journey in a far country returning home to Mother. Metropolitan PHILIP Saliba of the Antiochian Orthodox Christian Archdiocese of North America opened the door to us with the simple words of a loving father, "Welcome home." My parish was received into the Church on March 21, 1987, and I was ordained to the priesthood the following day.

The pilgrimage has been a long and hard one. Some who began the journey with us have chosen other paths. There have been frustrations and disappointments, along with the joys. There have been criticisms and misunderstandings; relationships have been lost, and relationships have been formed. If I were searching merely for a Church in which there are no conflicts, no issues to discuss, no fallible human beings, I certainly have not found it—and, I suspect, I never will on this side of heaven itself. As someone once said, "If I found the perfect Church I should never join it, because if I did, it would cease to be perfect."

What I have found is the Pearl of Great Price, the Kingdom of God. I have found the true Faith, the true Church of Christ, the true sacraments, and true communion with God. That is the measure of what God has given. And like the cost of that pearl to the merchant, it has cost me my life. It is exactly what I was looking for: a relationship with God, and an experience of Him in the Church that could command my fullest energies, my deepest sacrifice. Nothing phony, nothing shallow. My purpose is to know Christ truly, and to make Him known.

To be sure, our journey has really just begun. But something immeasurable has changed. Instead of looking for the house whose builder and maker is God, we are learning to live within it, until that day when we no longer see in a glass darkly, but face to face. And in that day we will fully know what it means for the Church to be "the fullness of Him who fills all in all," for "we shall be like Him, for we shall see Him as He is" (I John 3:2).

Chapter Three

FORBIDDEN GATES AND ROYAL DOORS

By Fr. Nicholas Sorensen

My senior high Sunday school class approached the front doors of the Roman Catholic church for an educational visit. We were excited, we were scared. As evangelicals, we were about to enter forbidden gates, to see with our own eyes what we had only heard about in sermons. This was the apostasy of Christianity, the whore of Babylon.

What I personally experienced that day was contact with something holy and reverent and awesome. For me Christianity would never again be just "Amazing Grace" and "What a Friend We Have in Jesus." Pastors in business suits behind centrally placed pulpits, with choirs, pianos, and organs visually dominating the front of the church, were no longer my vision. Although I certainly did not know it then, that day began my conversion to the Holy Orthodox Church.

The Thrill of Rebellion

It was the time of the hippies, civil rights marches, social experimentation, the insanity of the war in Vietnam. My college world was filled with flower children, with the thrill of rebellion against the establishment, and with the idealism of a place where love, gentleness, and peace ruled. I saw the church as fragmented and impotent. In fact, for six years, I rarely set foot in a church building and only infrequently read the Bible or prayed. I still considered myself Christian, but I certainly was not going the establishment route.

Christendom from my perspective was like a cafe. When I did get to church, I sampled from the menu. In high churches I was fascinated by vestments and liturgy, bells and incense, chanting and formal prayers. But in those churches which provided this fare, I sensed an intellectual arrogance which doubted the basic doctrines of Christianity as I understood them. The food was bittersweet. Occasionally I would attend churches which believed the fundamentals and upheld the Bible as the Word of God, but they were predominantly anti-liturgical. Something was missing. It was good food, but it didn't stick to my ribs.

As often happens at this age, I fell in love. Barbara was to be my companion, my friend, a faithful listener, my encouragement, my helper—my wife. She would walk side by side with me as we wandered through the labyrinth of ecclesiastical variety. Coming from a Grace Brethren background, she too was searching for something different, yet the same. We would often talk about our ignorance of the history of Christianity, our longing for more liturgical form, yet our desire for biblical Christian theology. No Christian denomination satisfied us. They all had something good but all seemed to have something missing.

Identifying with Luther

The war in Vietnam was raging, and I was eventually called up from ROTC to active duty at Wright-Patterson Air Force Base near Dayton, Ohio. Sampling from the cafeteria of American Christendom no longer appealed to us. Barbara and I decided to look seriously for a church home.

The Lutheran Church attracted me for several reasons, none of which were profoundly theological. The Protestant Reformation had been the only ecclesiastical root I really knew. Since the Lutheran Church was the first and eldest child of the Reformation, I sensed that joining her would be a return to the source—a return home.

Scenes from movies I had seen about the Reformation dominated my thoughts. I could see Martin Luther courageously standing before the Diet in Worms speaking the now-famous words, "My conscience has been taken captive by the Word of God, and I am neither able nor willing to recant, since it is neither safe nor right to act against conscience. God help me. Amen." The strains of "A Mighty Fortress Is Our God" echoed in my mind, and I felt this could be my church—strong, confessional, liturgical, a church not afraid to rebel against the errors of the established hierarchy.

The more I studied the Lutheran Church the more I was convinced that here was the perfect combination of doctrinal purity and liturgical worship. I could do no better than to be a Lutheran. The Roman Catholic Church was the more ancient and authentic body, but I saw Luther as purifying Rome from the changes introduced during the Middle Ages. Early Lutherans did not give up the liturgical practices of Rome. They simply corrected things that were theologically suspect. My desire for liturgy and for doctrine seemed to be fulfilled.

Completing my time in the Air Force, I was honorably discharged and returned to civilian life. I soon enrolled at Concordia Seminary in St. Louis to prepare for the Lutheran ministry. The next four years of intense theological training were stimulating. There was a reasoned answer to every question, a rational response to every doubt.

As we studied other denominations and Christian churches, great care was taken to define their doctrinal positions and practices and to show conclusively why they all were deficient when compared to Lutheranism. Roman Catholicism predictably was cast as the central villain, and Eastern Orthodoxy was given only superficial treatment. I got the impression Orthodoxy was merely a more esoteric version of Rome. This was, however, the first time in my life I had ever heard of the Orthodox Church. And I promptly forgot it.

Theology and Practice

In the summer of 1979, I was ordained as a pastor in the Lutheran Church Missouri Synod (LCMS). I saw almost immediately the academic precision of the seminary was not easily translatable to the local parish. My interest in liturgical renewal, which had begun in seminary, was also not accepted with joy by those in the pew. My use of authentic liturgical practices was grudgingly tolerated at best or branded as crypto-Catholic at worst.

Within three years of my first assignment, I was called as senior pastor to a large Lutheran church in western Iowa.

Now everything I had been taught and that I believed was tested in earnest. While I could enthusiastically embrace the version of Lutheranism which I was given in seminary, what I actually found in denominational practice was often very different and much more difficult to accept. The LCMS was moving rapidly away from the liturgical form characteristic of the Lutheran Church during the last half of the sixteenth century and towards a more informal, evangelical service.

I was fighting an uphill battle to *reintroduce* the common chalice, the sign of the cross, eucharistic vestments, and chanting. There were other issues that troubled me. I could not ignore the lack of apostolic authority, the failure to respect truly catholic traditions of the Church, the individualism, Protestant bibliolatry, inbred fear of ecclesiastical hierarchy, the instant "fix" ascribed to program after program.

Without doubt, the question which troubled me most involved identifying the true visible Church. Every denomination I had investigated claimed it was the true right Church and taught correct Christian doctrine. Each used the Bible to support its claim. For one, infant baptism was right; for another, wrong. One taught predestination, another, free will. Each interpreted Scripture according to its own isolated tradition. Which confession was apostolic? Which was most faithful to the teachings of our Lord? I had to know, and I had to be sure I belonged to the true historic Church.

It seemed reasonable that the older the tradition, the more reliable it would be. Yet no Protestant body (including the Lutherans) could claim a tradition which was more than 500 years old—just one-fourth of Church history!

It was during this time that I discovered the writings of Father Alexander Schmemann. Through this faithful priest I was introduced to the Holy Orthodox Church. My questions began to be answered. There was a fullness and unity in Orthodoxy that excited me. And there was an unsullied, easily supportable authenticity about Orthodoxy—an unbroken tradition dating from our Lord and His Apostles. No other Christian Church could legitimately claim that, not even Roman Catholicism.

I read more of the early Church Fathers. I continued to read about the sacraments, incense and chanting, fasting, rules of prayer, and monks. The pursuit of holiness was taken seriously. Most importantly, I found the early Church did not use the Bible as an exterior proof text for its theology, but rather obeyed the unbroken Apostolic Tradition handed down, guarded, and proclaimed by the Church. In fact, the Bible itself was authenticated, canonized, and subsequently understood and interpreted within that Tradition.

Thus, the Tradition of the One, Holy, Catholic and Apostolic Church was the ultimate authority by which doctrine and practice were judged—not an individually interpreted Bible. Neither Tradition nor the Bible taught *sola scriptura*. Yet the Bible was venerated, and believed. In addition, the doctrine of this early Church was not aberrant or strange to me; it was not liberal newspeak nor knee-jerk fundamentalism. Simply put, it was the Faith of the Apostles.

Reality Testing

But reading about a Church and experiencing it firsthand are often very different.

My very dear friend and colleague, Joseph Bragg—another Lutheran pastor who was walking the same spiritual path as I—had already made contact with a real, live Orthodox priest and with a group of former Campus Crusade staff members who had just been accepted into the Antiochian Orthodox Christian Archdiocese under Metropolitan Philip Saliba. With Joseph's help I was introduced to these men. They invited us to come and see Orthodoxy firsthand at a parish almost entirely composed of converts to Orthodoxy.

Nothing in my life had prepared me for what I would experience there. The church was filled. The people were respectful and focused on worship. From the beginning of the Liturgy, there was an overwhelming sense of the majesty and glory of God. But when the congregation began to sing "Holy God, Holy Mighty, Holy Immortal, have mercy on us," both Joseph and I broke into tears and remained so throughout the rest of the service. Our quest to find the Church was at an end. We had finally come into the presence of something holy and real—the One, Holy, Catholic, and Apostolic Church.

Following this wonderful experience, I was given several opportunities to visit older, more established Orthodox parishes. Here I again experienced the glory of God, but there was a marked difference from the initial experience. The Liturgy was beautiful, and I felt as if I were standing with all the saints and angels around the throne of God in heaven. But there was also a "culture shock" when faced with Eastern customs, ethnicity, and the partial use of a foreign language. My idealism was disturbed.

I was convinced the Orthodox Church had the right doctrine, the right practice, the right liturgy, and the right ecclesiology. But I had no desire to be Greek, Syrian, or Russian. I liked just being American! So without doubt, for me the greatest obstacle to entering the Orthodox Church was its strong ethnic identity.

Heading Home

That said, by the grace of God I was led to see again and again that within the Orthodox Church there were people who lived holy lives and who loved Christ and His Church even though they spoke a different language. I met extremely dedicated priests and deacons. I saw and felt the love of Christ in Orthodox communities where doctrine and practice were one. I came to believe that only Orthodoxy could draw all the wanderings of my spiritual journey together. Only in Orthodoxy would I experience true Christianity.

At first Barbara was very skeptical. To her it appeared I might be chasing rainbows again. Yet she assured me of her support and love even if I was going through "mid-life crisis." What amazes me is that she freely and lovingly followed me into Orthodoxy and into a change of life that not only exposed all of us to the fullness of the Christian Faith but also created many new challenges for her and for our four children.

In the spring of 1988, I resigned from the Lutheran ministry and moved my family to Franklin, Tennessee. There, under the guidance of Father Gordon Walker, we were eventually chrismated and accepted into the Antiochian Orthodox Christian Church under the visionary leadership of Metropolitan Philip. After a thorough course of study in Orthodox theology, history, and liturgy, and some good on-the-job training, I was ordained to the diaconate in 1989, and to the holy priesthood in 1990. My family and I had come home.

Well, almost.

Doubts

Finding the true visible Church was serious business for me. And when I found Orthodoxy, I felt my quest was over.

But it is hard to put aside a lifetime of questioning, skepticism, rebellion, and restlessness. Converts who have journeyed through the denominational mall, who always have another church to join if the one they are currently in doesn't work out, don't change overnight. The more deeply I got involved in Orthodoxy the more things I saw that disturbed me—things that were a part of the fallen nature of man rather than of the perfect holiness of the bride of Christ. The result was, I perfidiously resumed my quest—this time for a more Orthodox Orthodoxy!

Within the larger Orthodox community there are several groups who have broken canonical bonds with almost all other Orthodox Churches over what they call the heresy of ecumenism. These groups see the primary symptom of this heresy to be the rejection of the Julian calendar and the subsequent adoption of the more recent Gregorian calendar. They also pride themselves on strict observance of all the canons of the Church. These externals—purity of practice and of doctrine, old-world customs, their monastic disciplines—are very attractive to idealists who seek the perfect Church. The concept of a "holy remnant" standing against the establishment is also attractive to converts from conservative Protestant backgrounds. And it was attractive to me.

Once again, off I went to another group that would finally be the end of all my searching. I told myself this really wasn't Protestant church-hopping come back to haunt me. After all, I was still Orthodox; I just wanted to be *super* Orthodox. But once inside, I found myself greatly burdened. Along with zeal, I found a tremendous weight of legalism.

My tryst was brief. I left the new group and never returned. But where could I go? For awhile, I haunted the back pews of a Lutheran church in the area. It was comfortable to sing familiar hymns, but I was not at home. I even tried a Roman Catholic church.

During this same time, my family was falling apart because of my depression and lack of direction. The company I worked for was closed and I was unemployed. In the short space of six months, I had lost my church and my job. Would my family be next? I knew where home was. I knew what I had to do. But I was too ashamed to go back.

Home To Stay

But God did not abandon me. The very people I had turned my back on now reached out in love to me and to my family. With tears of true repentance I asked for their forgiveness, which was freely given. I wrote and asked Metropolitan Philip to forgive me for my willfulness and disobedience as a priest. I wanted only to return to the Antiochian Orthodox Church as an unworthy layman.

I will always remember the beautiful letter Metropolitan Philip wrote back to me. In it he forgave me and accepted me back as one of his priests. His last statement was the most touching. He wrote, "Welcome home, again!"

Since 1992, I have served as pastor of All Saints Mission in suburban Raleigh, North Carolina. I love my parish. I can still see the problems in Orthodoxy, but I know this is the Church. I know this is where I and my family belong. As an association of sinful human beings, the Orthodox Church is not perfect. But as the Bride of Christ, she is the pearl of great price. My journey to the Church, which started at the forbidden gates, has been completed at the Royal Doors. Here I stand. I can do no other!

Chapter Four

THE LAST TRAIN HOME

By Fr. Daniel Matheson

F all comes early in northern Manitoba. The scene is idyllic: cadmium aspens, ochre tamaracks, and the deep forest green of the jack pines—majestic symbols of the Canadian North. The last of the forest berries are gathered by the Objibway people.

But framed in this setting of unspeakable beauty, a quiet tragedy had unfolded. There, in a log cabin hidden deep in the woods, a tiny infant girl, the youngest of many children, died alone.

I was the United Church of Canada minister in a nearby mining town. I had arrived there a few months before from Halifax with my new clerical collar, a box of books, and all the confidence of a novice. Prayer book in hand, I conducted a funeral—a perfectly correct yet entirely inappropriate funeral—

while family and neighbors wept loudly.

"Why was no one with her?" was my silent cry to God. Half an hour later, frigid wind seemed to confirm the psychological horror that now chilled me. The cold cut deeper as I waited for the men of the encampment to finish driving the last of the nails into her tiny coffin. Inwardly I raged against God with the bitter anger of a man whose simplistic faith had been staggered by the harsh realities of life and death. My inner crisis had begun.

A Rebound in Faith

Six months later that crisis erupted. It was Holy Week, and as I studied the lectionary for the season I finally admitted to myself the truth that could no longer be denied: I believed none of it. Someone once said that it would have made no difference whether Jesus had died of a bad cold or on the cross. In my emptiness, I shared that sentiment.

Where was the unstudied faith that had impelled me into holy orders? "Naive," I called it now. Ruefully remembering my years in the divinity hall, I admitted to my wife, Vera, that only one sentence in the Gospel spoke to me with meaning: "They have taken away my Lord, and I know not where they have laid Him." I have no recollection of what I did that Easter Day.

I do, however, remember the following weeks vividly—grief for a lost faith, remorse for a hypocritical posture, and not the faintest idea that the answer to my dilemma lay in a single word: repentance. By the grace of God, one reality had been salvaged. I knew when my parents had brought me to the sacrament of baptism on an April day in 1916 they had given me to God. I had become His child, and He was my Father.

For the next four years my insistent prayer would be, "Father, I belong to You, straighten me out!" Strange things happened.

For example, there was the winter's day when Vera got up from the breakfast table and headed for the door to go to the school where she taught. As she turned her face up for a good-bye kiss, she dropped the happy bomb, "I'm pregnant!"

When I caught my breath, I ran up the stairs to my study singing the Magnificat. We named the baby *Mary*.

Mary was only four weeks old when God used her in a special way. Vera was nursing her in the ladies' room of the ferry that crossed the Bay of Fundy from New Brunswick to Nova Scotia. A cherubic priest, always half lost because of his poor eyesight, stepped cautiously into the room and asked if it was the men's room. A rather tense and very feminine "No!" did not faze him.

"Bless my soul," was his response, but then surprisingly he added "Are you nursing a baby? How beautiful!" Minutes later Vera greeted me on the deck, "You must meet the most amazing man I've ever talked to." He was Canon Quinton Warner, one of the founders of *Faith at Work*.

Using our daughter, Mary, as a launching point, he began talking about another Mary—the Mother of our Lord. Profoundly, yet simply, he confirmed to me that Mary's Child *is* indeed the Son of God, that everything He said *is* the Word of God, and that everything He did *is* the Love of God. My prayer was beginning to be answered!

I was sure I had arrived. At least I had made a start in the right direction. And Jesus never gained a fiercer disciple. From that point on, any pastor who came within my orbit received a free straightening out of his theology and adjustment of his pastoral practice—whether he wanted it or not.

Learning About Liturgy

During this time, my denomination had responded to an

invitation from the Anglican (Episcopal) Church to begin conversation leading toward union. They appointed me to the first committee in my conference. I suspect that they put me there for the same reason that people put bulldogs in warehouses overnight! I entered the situation with furious enthusiasm.

To my surprise, as I studied the Anglican liturgy, I found it did not differ greatly from my own. In fact, for the first time I discovered the true meaning of the liturgy I had been using for years. I learned that above all it was a celebration of our union with Christ. I also learned that, sadly, very few in my denomination shared this belief. Not to worry! I would enlighten them!

This proved to be a lonely endeavor. Oftentimes I found myself longing for a haven and a community of shared belief. Rome, I realized, was nearer than I had previously imagined. And far beyond Rome, I glimpsed the hazy and distant glory of the Eastern Orthodox Church.

As my study continued, at times I wished I had been dropped into this world from another planet and had the opportunity to choose the shape of my faith and worship. Which way would I go? The Orthodox way. But in reality, I was in "Union Station," not knowing which track to take. There were trains to Canterbury and Rome, but almost none to Constantinople; and when the infrequent one did come through, no one on board spoke my language!

Another Messenger

It was at this time another significant person came into my life, popular author and lecturer Bruce Larson. Had I known what I was in for, I would have avoided that April pastor's retreat in the Ottawa Valley. But once there, I had no graceful means of retreat.

Bruce's theme was: if your relationship with God is not

personal and joyful, the problem is quite likely to be found in your relationships with people. He convinced me. After some reflection, I realized the implications of his message. Spiritual pride was affecting my relationships with fellow Christians, and I would have to do something about it.

"God," I prayed desperately, "do I have to tell these other guys that I've thought I was smarter than they are?" Somewhere in the back of my head a voice answered, "No, you don't; you've already made that perfectly clear to them. Now you must ask them for help!"

"Yes Lord, if I must, I must!"

The next thirty-six hours were deathly; every person was kind, but I was humiliated. The second morning I rose early after a sleepless night. I had made a fool of myself, and I was sure it was Bruce Larson's fault.

Now I was headed for the Eucharist. How could I handle putting the bread in my neighbor's mouth with the words, "The Body of Christ broken for you, David or Archie or Matthew"? With all that was left of my shredded dignity, I chose my seat carefully and sat down. God had other plans.

The person sitting next to me suddenly got up and left, leaving the seat vacant. Bruce Larson came in and took the open chair. I was too proud to move.

The bread came. I made the worst action that I can imagine in any sacrament. Furiously I broke it and jammed it into Bruce's mouth, daring only to say, "the Body of Christ."

He was shocked by my anger. "Dan," he said, "look at me, and call me Bruce!"

I shall never forget looking into his face at that moment as I repeated the words, "The Body of Christ, Bruce, broken for you." And then Christ arose from the dead for me and brought me with

Him out of the gloom of a mere academic faith into the radiance of His glorious light.

Later that day, when I arrived home, Vera said, "What on earth happened to you?" I tried to tell her. "You'll never know how long I've prayed for this day!" she said.

Back on the Platform

And so, back to work. It wasn't easy. The United Church became rather uncomfortable for me—and with me. It is a very free Church, and for that I am indebted. I was free to find and use anything I could bring home from my forays into the "Holy Church throughout all the world." They, however, were also free to ignore my treasures.

I had had twenty good years, but now I was marching to a different drum. My theology was biblical, the Church's was liberal. I wanted to celebrate our union with Christ weekly, they wanted to have a kind of funeral for Him four times a year. I believed in His Real Presence, it seemed everyone else believed in His real absence.

Little by little I had become more and more alienated by liberalism. I was trying desperately to restore Jesus to His rightful place as the King and Head of the Church. It wasn't working.

My years were running out, and from where I stood I could see the shelf at the end of the corridor! My exit wasn't very dignified; one by one the doors closed, and I found myself, literally, on a cold and slushy sidewalk—alone. I was deeply distressed.

Surprisingly, I found myself singing, "All the way my Savior leads me, what have I to ask beside..." Somehow, I kept up the song. Thinking about my many years with the United Church, I asked myself, "Do I want to go back?" My answer, "No way!"

I found myself on the old station platform again, trains having left for Canterbury and Rome. It was likely too late for me. I was getting old, turning 70. At last, very unexpectedly, there came along a train heading all the way East toward Orthodoxy. The train was called the Evangelical Orthodox Church—and this time the crew spoke my language! Honestly, it was the last train out of the station.

The day was nearly spent for me, but I seized the opportunity and signed on. My colleagues had just made contact with Metropolitan PHILIP, head of the Antiochian Archdiocese in North America. By 1986, he extended to us an invitation to become Orthodox, and by 1987 we were on track.

Ultimately the small mission parish I pastored in Ottawa, Ontario, united with the much larger and older Saint Elijah Church in the city. Today I serve as acting pastor (I keep trying to retire, but to no avail!). I am constantly grateful to God for mercifully leading me back to the platform in time to catch that last train home. It took a lifetime to finally get on board. But this fullness of the Faith is worth every struggle and disappointment along the way.

Chapter Five

IT HAPPENED AT WESTERN CONSERVATIVE BAPTIST

By Fr. Thomas Renfree

I *f you weren't a Baptist what would you be?* I once posed the question to a fellow seminarian.

"I'd be ashamed!" was his response.

While my friend's degree of fervor was certainly not typical of every student at Western Conservative Baptist Seminary in Portland, Oregon, there was enough of such Baptist zeal to make a non-Baptist like myself occasionally feel out of place.

Yet in 1972 this seminary was the one I had freely chosen to attend (though at the time I did not believe in "free will"). Born and bred in the Methodist Church, I had come to the conclusion that the mainline Protestant denominations were theologically bankrupt. Having become active in college with Campus Crusade for Christ, I knew there was more to the Christian life than mere "Churchianity." Although I counseled others not to trust their feelings, I really felt the Lord was calling me into full-time Christian service.

Sold on Seminary

I seriously thought and prayed about going on staff with Campus Crusade, but somehow never felt convicted to take that step. If God was really leading me to full-time Christian service, some type of professional training would first be necessary. Besides, I had a genuine desire to further my understanding of God's Word and my faith. So I decided that seminary was the logical next step.

After considering several evangelical seminaries, I finally settled on Western Conservative Baptist. Western emphasized the things I wanted to learn, they seemed to believe the same doctrines we did in Campus Crusade, they offered a solid program of Bible, theology, and practical courses—and they didn't get upset if you went to movies! What more could any seminarian ask for?

From the moment I set foot on campus I loved it. I really looked forward to my first day of classes and relished the thought of getting an arsenal of biblical ammunition so that I could successfully witness to all those Catholics and other liturgical types who say they are sincere Christians but really aren't. I clearly remember my thoughts on the first day of class: "I know we evangelicals are right. Now I'm going to find out why."

Looking back, I have to say that those three years at seminary were some of the most valuable of my life. Since I was almost biblically illiterate when I started, I soaked up everything like a sponge, especially Bible classes. It was all so new to me. I loved each hour in the classroom. I even loved the Greek class that started promptly at 7:30 A.M. every morning (and where, if I walked in at 7:32, the professor would stop class and say: "Good *afternoon* Mr. Renfree"). I knew these classes were preparing me to be a "worker who does not need to be ashamed, rightly dividing the word of Truth" (II Timothy 2:15).

Seminary gave me something for which I will always be indebted: such a love for the Bible that ultimately I could never be content outside of the New Testament Church. It gave me the tools to study God's Word, to discover the truth, and the desire to find and to serve that Church which Christ had established through His Apostles. As ironic as it now seems, a Baptist seminary actually prepares a serious student to become Orthodox.

I graduated from seminary convinced that evangelicals don't believe the Bible *enough*. In practice most evangelicals I encountered were very selective in their approach to Scripture— that is, they believed the whole Bible except for those passages which ran contrary to their presuppositions. Even then they would never come right out and say they rejected those passages. They just managed to effectively change the meaning by fancy interpretive footwork. Let me give some examples which I encountered in the course of my seminary training.

1. Bible Interpretation

At seminary I was taught to confess with Saint Peter that "no prophecy of Scripture is of any private interpretation ..." (II Peter 1:20). But in practice our system of hermeneutics or biblical interpretation was based upon a relatively modern theory. It emphasized that every Christian has the right and the responsibility, under the guidance of the Holy Spirit, to interpret the Bible for himself. That sounds good at first—

until you start counting Protestant denominations!

I came away from seminary frustrated that there were so many different interpretations of the same Scriptures among seemingly godly people, all of whom claimed the leading of the Holy Spirit. These differences were not over minor points of doctrine, but major issues. Was the Holy Spirit divided? Or did the hermeneutic I was being taught make every Christian a Protestant Pope, each one speaking "infallibly" about what the Bible says?

2. Holy Tradition

My fellow seminarians and I were always quick to point out that we believed in the Bible rather than tradition. But we failed to distinguish between the "traditions of men" criticized by our Lord, and the Holy Tradition of God which the Bible itself commends (see Saint Paul's exhortations in II Thessalonians 2:15, 3:6).

In all my years of seminary I don't recall ever hearing anything good said about Holy Tradition. I now believe this is one of the glaring omissions in evangelical seminary education. Because many evangelicals have such an aversion to the "T" word (that's "Tradition," not "Tithing"), they have effectively denied the vital role of godly Tradition in the formation and transmission of the Holy Scriptures themselves. Without Tradition we would not have the Bible.

I remember one day in theology class a student asked the professor: "If we accept the decision of the Church at the Council of Carthage (fifth century) which settled the New Testament canon of Scripture, why do we reject that same Church which made the determination of the books of the Bible?"

"A good question," responded the professor, "one to which we Baptists have no good answer."

3. The Sacraments

To their credit, the professors at Western strongly confessed the truth of the Incarnation of Christ. Practically, however, they denied the sacramental nature of life inherent in the fact that God the Son became fully human. In their denial of the sacraments, of icons, of the historic liturgical worship of the Church, I believe they unwittingly fell into a form of gnosticism which elevates the "spiritual" realm and downplays the physical creation as a means of God's grace.

The doctrine of God's grace was taught, but the biblical vehicles of grace were denied—vehicles such as the waters of baptism (in spite of historic Church teaching on passages such as John 3:5; I Peter 3:21; Acts 2:37,38; Romans 6:3,4; Titus 3:4,5). They taught us about the Lord's Supper, but spiritualized the meaning out of Jesus' words recorded in John 6 ("Whoever eats My flesh and drinks My blood has eternal life . . .") by making these words merely symbolic.

Evangelicals do honor at least one sacramental act—the preaching of the Word—and in that sacrament they excel. Western Seminary had several fine courses in homiletics. It only had one "elective" class, however, on biblical worship. Because they have neglected to formulate any kind of sacramental theology, evangelicals accept by default a form of worship based upon the entertainment and/or lecture models of our modern age rather than upon any kind of biblical model.

A few of my professors decried the emptiness of evangelical worship. One even admitted that worship in the Baptist Church had degenerated into "the professionals performing for the pew potatoes." But no one seemed willing to consider the rich tradition of the Church with regard to liturgy which, when combined with good biblical preaching, constitutes true Orthodox worship.

I graduated from seminary in 1977, aware that I still had much to learn. After ministering for a couple of years in a Baptist Church, my misgivings about Baptist theology and practice proved too troublesome, so I left to begin an "Independent Bible Church." The stated goal of those of us who started this Church in the living room of one of our homes was "to be like the New Testament Church."

To be honest, we really had no idea what the New Testament Church was like in practice. Despite my seminary education, I was still very ignorant in the area of Church history. It was, in fact, the study of Church history which over a period of several years brought us to the doors of Orthodoxy.

For a long time I had the mistaken belief that evangelical Protestants preached better, worshipped better, sang better, evangelized better, and knew the Bible better than any Christians since the Apostles. Now I came to realize that, in fact, everything true and good that evangelicals believe and practice we received from the Orthodox Church. Since we shared their goals and direction, our little house-church joined the Evangelical Orthodox Church, and the rest, as they say, is history. Actually, it was just the culmination of a very exciting journey which led us into a new beginning in Orthodox Christianity.

Like all other seminaries, Western Conservative Baptist Seminary had its strengths and its weaknesses. Given the limitations of a divinity school to prepare one fully for life in the Church, I suppose we should not expect too much from any one school. However, as long as Western continues to emphasize absolute fidelity to the Word of God, I expect that I will not be the last student to emerge from its classrooms into the arms of the Orthodox Church.

After all, in becoming Orthodox I was only doing what in one form or another I was taught to do at every class I ever attended at Western Conservative Baptist Seminary: "Contend earnestly for the Faith which was once for all delivered to the saints" (Jude 3).

Chapter Six

A CONVERT FROM WITHIN

By Fr. Frank Milanese

L et me say right off, I'm probably the one person in this book who didn't *start* his Christian life as a Protestant. I was born and raised within the Greek Orthodox Church, moved toward Protestantism as an adult, but now serve as a priest within the Greek Orthodox Archdiocese of North and South America. Then why am I writing this chapter for a book about Protestant ministers who have become Orthodox?

Because I still have a convert's heart.

Struggling with My Faith

Like many who are born and raised within a particular Christian expression, I did not have a solid grasp of what it means to be a follower of Jesus Christ as a young person. In addition to the usual hurdles and perplexities confronting any young, twentieth-century Christian, I also faced a serious language barrier: the Orthodox parishes I participated in as a child held their services entirely in Greek. As with most Americans, I spoke only English.

During my high-school years I attended Sunday school, participated as an altar boy, and sang in the choir (phonetically, of course). All of this experience gave me a closeness to my Eastern Orthodox heritage. Unfortunately, the one thing it did not give me was an intimate, understandable relationship with Jesus Christ. I am not saying He was absent from my life, or that I didn't know of Him. I did not, however, have an intimate communion or *relationship* with Him, in the words of Saint Ephraim, as "Lord and Master of my life."

Although I graduated in the top twenty-five percent of my high-school senior class, I saw my grades slip drastically during my freshman year of college. Since my only real goal in life at this time was to get a college degree, this poor showing shook my academic confidence greatly. I changed my major twice before finding an academic area in which I felt productive and able. Spiritually, I wondered what life held besides the struggle for good grades and the illusive dream of a productive career.

At about this time, I first became aware of the effect Jesus Christ could have on a person's life through the conversion of a family friend. This conversion evoked a tremendous change in this man—in fact, he went on to become an evangelist. As I listened to his testimony something burned inside me. I can remember crying like a baby, and not knowing why. I said many prayers and made many commitments, but somehow nothing ever changed. I felt lost and left on my own to struggle with my Christian life.

It was not until I was introduced to the ministry of the Holy

Spirit through an evangelical campus group that I began to see a grounding of my faith, and positive and active results of my prayers. As I called upon the Holy Spirit to strenghten me, both my outlook and my academic pursuits took a dramatic change for the better.

As I continued growing closer to God and moving through the remainder of college, I maintained my sacramental participation in the Greek Orthodox Church although I also attended an evangelical parish for its biblical teaching. It was while listening to the Protestant pastor preach a sermon and hearing his references to *the Greek texts* as a way to understand the New Testament, that I began thinking anew concerning my own heritage. Frankly, I had wondered if God was still active within the Orthodox Church.

When I went to examine the texts of the liturgical services of my Church, I found that not only were they "spirit-filled," but nearly ninety-five percent were taken directly from the Scriptures. With great joy I discovered that God *was* present within my Church—and had been all along. At the same time, I grew furious that no one had told me in plain English what a treasure this Eastern Orthodox Faith contained. I also knew I was not alone. Many of my Orthodox brothers and sisters in Christ had been kept in the dark because of liturgical language barriers and the lack of translated texts.

My heart went out to other young people like myself who were struggling with their faith, feeling alone as I had, not knowing what their Church had to offer. If only God could send someone to help them.

Enter: Campus Crusade

Upon successful completion of my undergraduate work, I

was accepted on the full-time staff of Campus Crusade for Christ. I moved to Crusade's international headquarters in San Bernardino, California, where I worked first as a computer operator, then as a systems programmer. During my two-and-a-half years on staff with this organization, I fully participated in the nearby Greek Orthodox parish, Saint Prophet Elias. I sang in the choir (still in phonetics), taught Sunday School, and acted as a youth advisor. Campus Crusade encouraged my active participation within the Greek community. They viewed me as an intercultural ambassador, since I had been raised in the Greek/American environment.

Throughout these years, God was actively preparing me for my ministry to come, although at the time I did not recognize this fact. The Bible-study techniques as well as the encapsulating of important doctrinal messages into "transferable concepts" gave me the tools I would later use to assist in the transmission of the Orthodox Christian message to youth and adults.

I also learned one other very important skill while on staff with Campus Crusade for Christ: recognizing the sovereignty of God through specific prayers and through seeing specific answers to those prayers. I did not know how important this would be until a few years later.

The Next Step

Campus Crusade was a stepping stone in God's plan for my life. Knowing He had blessed me with technical skills and abilities that I wanted to enhance and develop for His service, I returned home to West Virginia to pursue a graduate degree in computer science. As it turned out, however, my life's plans were to take several unexpected turns. The first came when, instead of going to graduate school, I accepted a job working at Mellon Bank in Pittsburgh, Pennsylvania, as a programmer/analyst.

At this point in my career, I still honestly thought that my life was beginning to settle down. I had been able to give a few years to active Christian service, I had a great job in a field that happened to be my favorite hobby, and the Greek Orthodox Diocese of Pittsburgh had a wonderful youth program that was actively experiencing God's blessing. I became very active with the youth and various Bible studies.

I truly believed that I would now be living within this basic framework for the rest of my life. Still, deep within my heart I knew something was lacking in my life. I wanted to be more active teaching the youth about their Faith. I wanted them to have the opportunity to know Jesus is active within the walls of an Orthodox Church and to learn they needn't go elsewhere to find out about Him. I wanted these young people to be able to draw upon the wealth of their own upbringing, and not feel the need to travel to foreign spiritual lands.

It soon became obvious that I would not accomplish these goals while still holding down a full-time job. So exactly one year after beginning my new position at Mellon, I gave my two-week notice and applied for seminary at Holy Cross Greek Orthodox School of Theology in Brookline, Massachusetts. I left a marvelous job with great potential, broke the lease on my apartment, completed my application information, moved back home to West Virginia, repacked for seminary, and was accepted for entry at the school—the day before I left for Massachusetts and Holy Cross. This all occurred within two weeks.

A Convert Still!

Four years later, in May of 1983, I graduated with a master of divinity degree from Holy Cross. I was married in 1985 and ordained in 1986. Since then I have served two years as an assistant priest gaining my initial parish experience, two years as the Director of Youth Programs for the Greek Orthodox Diocese of Pittsburgh, and then as associate pastor in a large Greek Orthodox parish in Ohio.

My convert's heart still burns with a yearning to do more each day than twenty-four hours will allow. I know I have found my true calling. Here in this ancient Church—a Church I had the privilege to have grown up in—I will serve my Lord and His people as long as He gives me strength.

As one with a true "convert's heart," I pledge myself to serve this Church, and to labor together with my brothers and sisters for her advancement in America.

Chapter Seven

ASBURY DREAMS AND ORTHODOX REALITIES

By Fr. Andrew Harmon

When as a theologically conservative layman in the United Methodist Church I first began to feel God's call into the ministry, Asbury Seminary in Wilmore, Kentucky, was the only school I seriously considered. Asbury is a non-denominational and conservative Wesleyan school which draws large numbers of more traditional and evangelical United Methodist ministerial candidates. Most United Methodist seminaries, on the other hand, are known to be hotbeds of heterodoxy.

Accordingly, I set off to Asbury and bluegrass country for what I now look back upon as a good three years of schooling with many valuable lessons. Asbury strongly emphasized adherence to the traditional beliefs of Christianity. This emphasis was doubly important, since most of us were headed for the pastorate in a denomination where being traditional was all but grounds for excommunication.

Asbury sought to retain the teaching of John Wesley, the founder of Methodism in eighteenth century England. In my research I began to discover Wesley believed many things modern Wesleyans either disbelieve or try to ignore—the real presence of Christ in the Eucharist, baptismal regeneration, and even the ever-virginity of Mary. I also discovered Wesley studied seriously the writings of the ancient Greek Church Fathers.

Finding the Fathers

This discovery led me to dig a little deeper into the Church Fathers myself, and in particular, the Orthodox Church. My graduate work in Russian history had already made me aware of Orthodox Christianity. But for a number of reasons, I had never seriously considered it for myself. Now I approached the matter far more seriously.

Without question, the Orthodox Church had stood the test of time—almost two-thousand year's worth to be exact. Protestantism, on the other hand, had fragmented into theological anarchy and ecclesiastical chaos after only a few centuries. Even the evangelical movement compromised away much it had stood for under the pressures of increasingly secular culture. And the modern Wesleyan folks seemed to want to ignore large factors in traditional Christianity (such as the sacraments) that had been enormously important to Wesley himself.

So I took some courses in Church history and the early Fathers and did some independent study as well. I became more and more convinced that the ancient traditions of the Church contained much that modern Protestantism had overlooked. Still I wasn't totally sold. This transition would be a slow and gradual process. By the time I reached graduation from Asbury I was not yet to the point of jumping into the Orthodox Church.

Frankly, my goal at that time was to work within the Protestant world to bring it more into line with the teachings and practices of ancient Christianity. Like most others at Asbury, I thought and hoped that Methodism would yet be recaptured from the forces of modernity. So my wife, Bonnie, our first child, and I headed out into the parish ministry full of zeal, ready to do battle against heterodoxy and save souls for Christ. And I, due to my new-found love for the Fathers and Orthodoxy, hoped to steer things in a more traditional, patristic direction.

Seminary had gotten me started positively on the road to Orthodoxy. From the other direction, my denomination would now give me the final push!

The Methodist Pastorate

My three years as a Methodist pastor were exciting, fulfilling, and just plain fun. It was a great job! But, serving a parish in a mainline Protestant denomination can also be a tremendously disillusioning experience. The power structure exerted consistent pressure for us to conform with whatever innovative trends were going on in the denomination. An Asbury training was considered fine as long as it contributed to church growth and success—but not if it questioned or resisted errant teaching within the denomination.

Two factors, in particular, soon convinced me that my Asbury dreams of reforming and revitalizing Methodism were only illusions. First, I became aware of how many Asbury grads had succumbed to pressure and compromised their beliefs. Many of them were at various stages of crossing over into doctrinal defection. This frightened me. How could I know I wouldn't eventually do likewise?

I remember a visit to my home by a friend and fellow seminary grad who, like me, had now been pastoring for about two years. We hadn't seen each other much since seminary and so were sharing our experiences as pastors. My friend had been a very principled and theologically astute fellow at seminary— one who knew what he believed and had no intentions of caving in to pressures to change his beliefs.

Two years in the pastorate had changed him drastically. He now thought those who had abandoned scriptural beliefs were "okay." He didn't agree on everything but could happily work together with them and considered them to be good Christians. This came as a real shock to me. I recall thinking, "This may be the way I will soon talk, too." After all, who was I to be strong enough to stay true to what I believed if others were wavering? This helped convince me that I needed to make a drastic change.

A second factor helped convince me my Asbury dreams were really illusions. One of the big selling points for evangelicals to stay and minister in liberal denominations is the hope that such a person can always make a mark for Christ and steer people in the right direction in a local congregation even if the denomination is rife with heresy.

Although this argument contains a measure of truth, a big hole became quickly obvious in my particular setting. I pastored a parish in a coal-mining boom-town in western North Dakota. The nature of much of the work there (power plant construction) made for a very transient population as people moved in and out of town for new job assignments.

God blessed our work in being able to lead some people to Christ for the first time and to help others to strengthen their

Christian commitment. With love and orthodox scriptural teaching these people began to grow in their spiritual lives. Unfortunately, due to the transient nature of the town, many of these people would soon move somewhere else. Those who came to Christ in a Methodist Church would most naturally attend the Methodist Church in their new area. What kind of theology might this new Church be teaching? A great deal of good work could be undone very quickly and these new sheep lost forever.

So I found myself warning people who were moving to be very cautious about the Methodist Church in their new town. At times I even urged them to look into other denominations for a possible Church home.

This soon struck me as an absurd situation. How much revitalizing of the denomination would I accomplish by steering new converts away from our own Churches? Yet, what else could I do to protect these newborn spiritual children? Obviously, if I couldn't even recommend someone to attend another parish in my own denomination, the handwriting was on the wall for me as well. The time had come for me to reconsider the entire direction of my ministry.

Recapturing mainline Protestantism from modern unbelief appeared hopeless. Nudging Protestants towards more Orthodox beliefs seemed even more hopeless. After all, how much success could I expect in trying to convince someone of the communion of saints when half the pastors didn't even believe in the Resurrection of Christ?

During our years in the Methodist pastorate, my wife and I studied more about Orthodox Christianity and became increasingly convinced that the Orthodox Church was where we needed to be. As my Asbury dreams increasingly turned out to be unfulfilled, the reality of Orthodoxy grew more and more appealing.

Making the Move

In 1982 we left the United Methodist Church to become part of the Evangelical Orthodox Church, a group of people with backgrounds similar to ours who also had set their hearts towards the Orthodox Faith. In 1987, the Evangelical Orthodox Church was received into the Antiochian Orthodox Christian Archdiocese and I was ordained to the priesthood.

The years from 1982 on have definitely had their share of difficulties—relocation, job hunting—but it's all been more than worth it. The help and love we received when entering the Church was outstanding. Especially helpful were Father Joseph Olas and the wonderful people of Saint George Church in Indianapolis. Father Joe took me under his wing and graciously taught me how to be an Orthodox priest—after all, how much training in liturgics do you get in a Methodist seminary?

After a temporary one-year assignment of helping organize All Saints Mission in Bloomington, Indiana, I was appointed pastor of Saint Matthew Mission in suburban Cleveland. God has blessed Saint Matthew's richly. We've had good growth, we now own a building, and before too long hope to grow from "mission" status into a full-fledged parish. It's great to be back in full-time ministry after several years of secular work. And what a great group of faithful people the congregation of Saint Matthew's is!

Even if things had not turned out so well in terms of ministry—even if I could not have been ordained into the priesthood—I still would become Orthodox all over again. The Orthodox Christian Church is the Pearl of Great Price, and it is far better to be in it regardless of circumstances than to be in wonderful circumstances anywhere else. As Psalm 84:10 says, "I would rather be a doorkeeper in the house of my God than dwell in the tents of wickedness." The reality of Orthodoxy is far better than the illusions of life outside.

Thanks be to God for bringing us from mere dreams to reality!

Chapter Eight

THE PEARL OF GREAT PRICE

By Fr. Paul Waisanen

Some sociologists tell us we are products of our cultural heritage. I can agree only in part. We are not "products." We are "persons" who make real choices within our social heritage. Growing up as I did in the global village of the latter half of the twentieth century, those choices could be somewhat frightening.

Fortunately my parents gave me focus. We lived on poor farm land with a small house and a much larger barn in Northern Michigan, the "U.P." in Aura, a Finnish immigrant community. We learned Luther's catechism in the rural Sunday school where I went ten to twenty Sundays of the year.

I swore once in front of my mother when I was five. A quick slap on the mouth made a distinct impression concerning the ethics of speech. I don't remember blurting out a word like that again until after I had graduated from Bible college.

Through Vacation Bible School, and friendship with some young Christians in high school at L'Anse, Michigan, I came into contact with the Baptist Church. These were among the few Christians I met who lived life in an atmosphere of the love and joy of Jesus Christ. I liked that and I became one of them.

Bible School

Then came Bible college in Grand Rapids. There I discovered Christian doctrine, apologetics, principles of Bible interpretation, Greek, and the defense of the authenticity of the books of the Bible. This matter of authenticity was a bit of a shock. Previously I had been taught that the early Church had forsaken the New Testament Church (which had been basically Baptistic, of course) and became the horrible Roman Catholic Church, which along with Red China and Russian communism were the great enemies of Christ "in these last days." At college I was taught, by contrast, that Papias and Ignatius and Irenaeus and Eusebius were actually men to whom we could look for support, external witnesses to the reliability of the books of the Bible.

In philosophy classes I read Augustine and Thomas Aquinas and liked what I saw. I was given *Mere Christianity* by C. S. Lewis in my freshman doctrine class. Having felt the pain of Baptist sectarianism which kept my friends from seriously considering Christ in high school, I now began to see a glimmer of a Christianity without denominational barriers. I heard of the evangelicalism of E. J. Carnell and Billy Graham, and began to read *Christianity Today*. I began to gain a broader vision of basic Christianity. I even heard about Roman Catholics that were true Christians.

In the summer of 1963 I roomed with a Korean pastor from

Taegu, Chi Young Kim. He read the New Testament continuously from start to finish—at least 400 complete times by then—and challenged me to the core. He introduced me to Barth and Kierkegaard and Luther and Augustine and Calvin and Shakespeare and many others. He said, "You must understand Luther in his historical context." This made perfect sense. Luther was proclaiming his doctrine in a Roman Catholic Europe. He said, slowly, "Alan, you read 26 chapters of the New Testament every day, you will read all 260 chapters in ten days. If you read through the New Testament 100 times, you will be a better preacher than Billy Graham."

That fall I read the New Testament 15 times and it became very powerful to me. Mr. Kim had once said, "A young hoodlum told me, 'First I drink liquor, then liquor drinks liquor, then liquor drinks me.' So I read Bible, then Bible reads Bible, then Bible reads me." My theology began to crumble. Grace in the Bible was coupled with strenuous standards. Dispensational theology could not contain the Sermon on the Mount. Covenant theology could not contain the awesome sense of human responsibility which I found throughout the New Testament.

Kierkegaard pointed to the importance of "suffering" in the Christian life. He spoke mysteriously of the "old preachers" of Christianity which he read aloud on Sunday afternoons. But Kierkegaard did not have the full answer. He died issuing an attack on the local Danish Church. He left me swimming in subjectivity.

Seminary

Going on to Trinity Evangelical Divinity School in Deerfield, Illinois, I heard for the first time the reality of the eyewitness testimony of the Apostles to the Resurrection of Christ through

John Warwick Montgomery. "Jesus is the Messiah, Jesus is Lord, He is not here, He is risen." "That which our eyes have seen and our hands have handled." "This thing has not been done in a corner." Jesus authorized the written Bible and the Apostles. Therefore the Bible is the Word of God. I began to work out the development of the fundamental doctrines from this base: Creation out of nothing, man in the image of God, the fall into sin, the education of Israel, the virgin birth, the Person and work of Christ, salvation, the Church, the Last Things.

In Church history classes, I heard for the first time of "Eastern Orthodoxy" with keen but passing interest. Our conservative Presbyterian teacher said, "All of you are Low Church! You should realize that what Cyprian said is true, 'Outside the Church there is no salvation!' "

I said to myself, "Of course, outside the 'invisible' Church there is no salvation." But that is not what Cyprian meant!

"If anyone knows that Jesus Christ commanded baptism and refused to be baptized, then he is outside the Church and is not a Christian," the teacher said. "Baptism is how you enter the Church." My perspective was becoming more concrete. This is essential to the most basic Christianity. It is solid. There is no "mere Christianity" apart from the Church or baptism.

He toppled my presuppositions again when he said, "The Roman Catholic Church was the True Church until it formally cursed the Gospel at the Council of Trent." I have since come to believe that it lost that status when it officially cursed the Eastern Church and the original Nicene Creed without addition.

This was a revelation to me. How can we avoid the splits in our Churches? By not separating ourselves from the True Church. Ever! If that which once was the True Church officially rejects the truth of Christ in some essential way then it is no longer the Church until it repents.

The Pastorate

This vision of the Church became my guide while I pastored a small country Church in rural Tampico, Illinois, and when I moved with my young family to California looking for answers among the "Body Life" Christians and the charismatics. Still feeling I was a Baptist, I was ordained by the Southern Baptists in 1979.

When two fellow-elders and I began our new mission we couldn't exclude those baptized as infants from full participation in our Church, so we couldn't remain Baptist. We became Emmanuel Community Church. We wanted to be biblical, expressing historic Christianity, and alive in the Spirit.

When we met Father John and Isabel Anderson and the Holy Transfiguration Orthodox Mission and its people, and saw 2000 years of faithfulness to the Gospel in its liturgy, Creed, and sacramental life, I could see no grounds for anyone to be a Christian and be separate from this Church. Whenever in the history of the Church anyone denied this Gospel, such as Arius, this Church had separated them from its fellowship.

For me, I could stand outside no longer. I was chrismated into the Orthodox Church by His Grace Bishop Basil (OCA) on the Feast of the Three Hierarchs, January 30, 1982. I was tonsured reader in 1983, attended Saint Tikhon's Seminary during 1988-89, and was ordained priest July 21, 1991. Today I pastor Holy Transfiguration Orthodox Mission Parish in La Habra, California.

I believe that the Orthodox Church has come to America, even in all its ethnic clothing, so we American Christians who are seeking genuine Christianity can find it in its most fundamental and concrete sense. We may need to sell off some of the extra trappings which have developed in the years since Rome divided from the Orthodox Church, and since the Protestant Church divided from Rome, but the pearl of liberty in Christ is worth the price.

This pearl, the Orthodox Church, includes two thousand years of living tradition of the people of God since Christ's Resurrection, and the Apostles and saints who have lived and proclaimed it. Having found it, I thank God for leading me here by way of caring parents, sincere Christian friends, and a Protestant education which opened my understanding to a reality beyond its own horizons—the reality of the historic Church, the true Pearl of Great Price, as it has been expressed throughout the ages.

Chapter Nine

AFTER FORTY YEARS

By Fr. Alister Anderson

I
t happened in the summer of 1953.

A resident at the Graduate School of Theology at the University of the South, Sewanee, Tennessee, I had some late-evening reading to do in the library. There was no one else in the building except the librarian, who had already begun to close down for the night.

Suddenly I had the strangest feeling that someone was watching me. The more I tried to read, the more this sense persisted.

The Portrait
Finally I felt compelled to rise from my chair and walk over to a dimly lighted area where I thought those unseen eyes might

be. When my sight adjusted to the shadows, I saw on the wall above me a large portrait of a bishop of the Episcopal Church. I read his name on the brass plaque below.

Hugh Miller Thompson (1830-1902)
Second Bishop of Mississippi

I still recall vividly the excitement that swept over me. I re-read the plaque and recognized this name as one I had occasionally heard mentioned during my childhood and adolescence. My great-grandfather, Hugh Miller Thompson, was this Episcopal bishop.

I never realized he had been at Sewanee. My parents rarely talked about him or, for that matter, about my grandfather, Frank Thompson, an Episcopal priest who served as a chaplain in the Navy for forty years. Instead, they wanted me to follow in my father's footsteps and become a naval officer in the regular Navy.

As I looked at the portrait, I felt a keen disappointment that my parents had not told me about my ancestors. I was equally disappointed in myself for failing to do my own family research. These feelings, however, abated quickly through the pride and joy I felt in knowing I was descended from such highly distinguished clergymen. For the first time in my life I realized my beloved ancestors had been calling me through prayer to ministry in the Episcopal Church. The Christian reality of the communion of the saints had bound them to me in a spiritual union that transcends all earthly time and space.

From the Navy to Seminary

My adult life began during World War II. I graduated from

the U.S. Naval Academy at Annapolis, Maryland, and was assigned to a destroyer in the Pacific Ocean. During those years, performing my duties in the naval profession, I began to grow increasingly restless. In time I became convinced that my unrest resulted from a spiritual hunger which heretofore I had not taken seriously.

Finally in the fall of 1947 I resigned from the Navy and applied to seminary. Since my parents were not members of any particular denomination, I decided to go to Union Theological Seminary, an inter-denominational institution located in the heart of New York City.

It was at Union, through the influence of several members of the faculty, that I sought ordination in the Episcopal Church. There I learned about the Anglican Mass, the seven sacraments, the doctrine of the Church rooted in the Holy Scriptures, the Creeds, Holy Tradition, and the writings of the Church Fathers as defined by the seven Ecumenical Councils of the undivided Church. I was particularly inspired by two Protestant theologians, Dr. Paul Scherer and Dr. Reinhold Niebuhr, to preach Christ crucified and risen from the dead.

I was also inspired by two Episcopal theologians, Dr. Walter Bowie and Dr. Cyril Richardson, to love the doctrine of the One, Holy, Catholic, and Apostolic Church and to believe and celebrate that doctrine in the offering of the Holy Mysteries through the Anglican liturgy.

During this same time I was fortunate to hear several lectures by the renowned Orthodox theologian, Father Georges Florovsky, who taught at Saint Vladimir's Seminary directly across the street. In those days there was great hope among many Episcopalians that the Anglicans and the Eastern Orthodox might effect a mutual recognition of ecclesiastical orders with some form of inter-communion.

The Middle Way

In 1951, I was ordained a priest by the Episcopal Bishop of Maryland and went to my first parish convinced that I must preach and teach the *via media*—the middle way. Many of the clergy and laity in those days felt the Anglican Communion might be the only means by which both the evangelical and the catholic doctrines of the Church could be united. We believed such a middle way could hold in tension a union of Churches through comprehensiveness without compromise.

The idea of *via media*, first set forth by the Anglican Divines of the sixteenth and seventeenth centuries, and later expounded by Father John Henry Newman, offered the hope of eventually leading us eastward from Canterbury and Geneva to Constantinople.

The Church experienced explosive growth in the years immediately following World War II. In just two years I baptized nearly three hundred children and adults in my parishes. Sadly, this phenomenal growth ended just as quickly as it had begun. The poisonous seeds of secular humanism, outlined in the American Humanist Association's *Humanist Manifesto* in 1933, took root in our seminaries. In just a few years many bishops, clergy, and laity began to look to the secular culture for inspiration and guidance, and they imbibed deeply its mores and values.

The Viet Nam Years

Fortunately, the years between 1956 and 1977 found me somewhat protected from this tragic deterioration of Church doctrine and moral values. I had volunteered to serve as a chaplain in the U.S. Army, and was not forced by the Bishop of the Armed Forces to use the new Episcopal liturgy and accept the avant-garde theological ideas and mores in vogue in the Church.

My years as a chaplain were the most challenging and personally satisfying I had experienced until I embraced Orthodoxy. I ministered to men in combat during times of war, and to both men and women and their families during times of peace. This ministry brought me into close contact with all sorts and conditions of men. I experienced the joy of being needed and appreciated as a priest, and I was given the opportunity to share in every facet of their lives.

I frequently encountered Orthodox Christians who had been told by their priests back home to seek out an Episcopal chaplain if he or she could not find an Orthodox priest. I therefore met and came to know many Orthodox soldiers and their wives during my twenty-one years of service. Sadly for the Episcopal Church, this cooperative practice was discontinued. Heretical teaching and the collapse of biblical morality in large segments of the Anglican Communion made any form of on-going ecumenical dialogue and inter-communion with the Orthodox impossible.

When I retired from the Army Chaplain Corps, I had hoped to serve in parishes where I could stem the advance of the humanistic teachings which had engulfed my Church. I wanted to teach the faith and doctrine of the Anglican Divines and uphold the ancient Christian truth *lex credendi est lex orandi:* the law of belief is the law of prayer. After laboring in a parish for seven years, I finally had to concede this premise was no longer feasible in the Episcopal Church. The bishops demanded all parishes use the new Prayer Book and a female minister was sent to be a "priestess" in the parish where I served.

Like so many priests, I asked to be relieved of my pastoral responsibilities in the Episcopal Church and informed the bishop that I was being received into one of several continuing Episcopal Churches which were attempting to maintain traditional Anglican doctrine and worship. I had hoped the Anglican Catholic Church, into which I had been received as a priest and served for six years, could remain a truly "remnant" Church until such time that the arrogance and folly of the present leadership of the Episcopal Church could be replaced, and the essential truths of Anglican faith and worship would coalesce around the faithful remnant core.

Sadly, even this hope proved to be in vain. The continuing Anglican/Episcopal Churches I encountered disagreed openly over doctrine and ecclesiastical polity. Rather than preserving unity and strength within the traditional Anglican Communion, they simply divided and separated into more and more Church bodies.

So it was that with great heaviness of heart I had to admit to myself that the Church of my ancestors had abandoned much of her biblical, theological, liturgical, devotional, and moral foundations. I had come to the time when I had to make the very difficult decision to leave behind me all that had been so familiar for so long.

Help from Haiti

In 1988, I renewed an old friendship with the Right Reverend Michael Graves who is an Orthodox missionary priest in Haiti and the vicar general of the Orthodox Church in the Caribbean. He had been my acolyte in an Episcopal Church in New Jersey, and had always said my ministry as rector there inspired him to study for the priesthood.

I called Father Michael to ask about becoming an Orthodox priest. He explained what I should do, and in the process introduced me to the writings of Bishop Kallistos Ware, Father Alexander Schmemann, Father Anthony Coniaris, and Father Alexey Young—all of whom intensified my belief in the Orthodox Christian Faith. Through our prayers, correspondence, occasional meetings, and his gentle, loving persuasion, I knew that historic Orthodox Christianity was the only way for me.

In the end, there was only one thing that held me back from embracing Orthodoxy. For me, it was not the so-called "ethnic difference," which unfortunately does turn some people away from the Church. It was not reluctance or sadness in setting aside the magnificent Anglican liturgy. It was, rather, the fact that my admiration for the writings of Saint Thomas Aquinas had occluded and eclipsed my deeper understanding of the early Church Fathers.

In describing the results of the fall of man, for example, Aquinas proposed that while the will of man was corrupted, his intellect was not corrupt. The power of man's intellectual reasoning is elevated to such a lofty height in Aquinas' teaching, people are seduced to think they can supplant God's revelation with human reason.

Saint Thomas inadvertently opened the door to the error of the Greek philosopher Protagoras who said, "man is the measure of all things." This explains why so many people believe Christian truth need no longer be tied to revelation but can be mixed with the teachings of non-Christian philosophers. In my studies, I was both inspired and comforted to realize that there never needed to be a Reformation in the Eastern Orthodox Church because she believes today the same things that Jesus said and did when He lived in human flesh among us.

After an inspiring week in Haiti, where I observed the profound influence of the Orthodox Church among many people, I asked Father Michael where I could receive instruction and chrismation. He sent me to the Very Reverend George Rados, pastor of Saints Peter and Paul Church in Bethesda, Maryland. Father George's kindness, spiritual guidance, and thorough instruction encouraged me to petition the hierarchs of his Church for ordination.

His Eminence Metropolitan PHILIP granted my petition and Father George's request that I be ordained to assist him at Saints Peter and Paul. I was ordained to the holy priesthood by His Grace Bishop ANTOUN, January, 1992. I have been welcomed home. My forty years of wandering in what became an ecclesiastical wilderness is over. Now I have begun a new and wonderful pilgrimage in Orthodoxy not only with Saints Peter and Paul, but with Saints Ignatius, Gregory, Basil, John Chrysostom, Barbara, Thekla, Mother Maria Skobtsova, and many others.

In January of 1992, shortly after my ordination, we had the joy at Saints Peter and Paul to host the chrismations of a group of former Presbyterians and the ordination of their pastor, Kenneth Hines. On that same day, Dr. Patrick Reardon, an Episcopal theologian and former priest, was ordained to the Orthodox priesthood, and Dr. Ray Stephens, an educator from Virginia and a former Roman Catholic, was ordained deacon to head up a convert community in Virginia Beach. The list goes on.

I say this very seriously: somehow I sense that set of eyes in the library at Sewanee is taking note. I believe that my great-grandfather, and my grandfather, are cheering me on and praying for my well-being as an Orthodox priest. For I am truly seeking to follow in their footsteps, to worship Christ within His Church, and to serve Him there with all my heart and soul.

Chapter Ten

BACK TO PENTECOST

By Fr. Timothy Cremeens

From early childhood I knew I would one day serve God as a "preacher." I committed my life to Christ in my teens and was baptized in the name of the Holy Trinity. At this time God reconfirmed His call on my life to preach the Gospel.

In the Wesleyan-Holiness Church I attended with my family, the first step one took to enter the ministry was to study at a Bible college. By the time of my high-school graduation, I had become active in the Pentecostal/charismatic movement. So I searched for a Bible college based on Pentecostal theology and experience. In the fall of 1979 I entered Zion Bible College in East Providence, Rhode Island, to begin studies for the ministry.

Zion College

Founded in 1924, Zion was uniquely run on the "Faith" principle. Simply put, this principle states that the college will not charge its students room, board, or tuition, but the faculty, staff, and student body are to pray that God will touch the hearts of His people to give financially to the college and support its needs. Interestingly, Zion has followed this policy for over sixty years, and closed each fiscal year in the black.

Due to this policy, and the college's Pentecostal theology, the program highly emphasized prayer, and seeking God to be filled with the Holy Spirit to receive His power to be witnesses for Christ. While most of the classes centered on subjects like systematic theology, Church history, and Bible (the Scripture classes took up the bulk of the curriculum), all these classes were geared towards personal spirituality. As a Pentecostal/charismatic college, Zion stressed that each student should have a personal "born-again" salvation experience as well as a personal "baptism in the Holy Spirit." In most cases, this baptism was to be followed by "speaking in tongues" as a sign that one had received this Holy Spirit baptism.

The Church history classes, which I especially enjoyed, followed the basic evangelical approach: after the conversion of Constantine in the early fourth century, the Church went into apostasy. It lost the Apostolic faith and power it had been given at Pentecost. Tradition replaced Scripture, causing all sorts of errors—such as liturgy, bishops, and veneration of the saints—to creep into the Church. True Christianity wasn't restored until the Reformation, and then only partially. With the Pentecostal revivals of the early twentieth century the power of the Holy Spirit and His gifts as manifested in the Book of Acts were at last revived in the Church in these last days before Christ's return.

Basic Questions

The great majority of the teachers and students were sincere, dedicated Christian people. But as I studied the history of the Church, and the doctrine of the Holy Spirit, many questions came to my mind. If the Bible is the only rule of faith for the Church, and the Holy Spirit was filling the Pentecostal believers, as I had been taught, why were there such diverse interpretations of the Scriptures even among the Pentecostals who shared the same experience? If the early Apostolic Church is the model of contemporary Church life, due to its pristine spiritual state and manifestation of charismatic gifts, how did the Church grow and maintain herself without each primitive believer carrying around a personal Bible to read and study? Lastly, was the worship of the early Church *really* a free-for-all charismatic meeting without any form or structure? I wasn't satisfied by the answers given in class.

Not knowing where to go to find the answers, I continued at Zion and graduated in the spring of 1981, going on to be ordained in the Assemblies of God, the largest Pentecostal denomination in the United States, and to pastor four congregations. All the while I continued to study and seek for the answers to my questions.

My own charismatic experience brought me to look at the doctrine of the Holy Spirit very seriously, along with the worship of the Church that was to be inspired by the Holy Spirit. In harmony with Pentecostal teaching, however, the Bible was the only textbook I searched. As a pastor, those questions resurfaced over and over.

Zion taught me to pray and seek the guidance of the Holy Spirit, who would lead me into all truth. So I did just that. To make a long story short, I finally began to study the early Church, beyond the pages of the Book of Acts. In turn this led me to the writings of the Fathers and the later Christian literature.

Critical Conclusions

I came to the conclusion the Church was able to teach the truth and grow in those first centuries because the Holy Spirit was present within the Church, "the pillar and ground of the truth" (I Timothy 3:15). Each believer filled with the Spirit was in communion with Christ and His Holy Church, and the Spirit had passed on from generation to generation the correct understanding of the Apostolic Faith (II Timothy 2:2). The Scriptures were not open to just any interpretation, but were interpreted by the Church as a whole. Holy Tradition, the very thing spurned by Pentecostalism, had protected, preserved, and continued the Apostolic Faith in the Church by the ministry of the Holy Spirit. This Apostolic Faith, this Holy Tradition, was still being passed on and kept intact without addition or deletion in the Holy Orthodox Church.

It was very encouraging to learn the Orthodox Church does not deny the charismatic gifts but actually embraces them, and by her structure and theology protects them from being abused and misused. Many saints, such as Saint Simeon the New Theologian and Saint Seraphim of Sarov, received wonderful charismatic giftings, and along with them left much wisdom to the Church on how these gifts were to be acquired and function within the Church for her edification.

My discovery of the Orthodox Church also helped to clear up another issue in my life: the issue of worship. Some elements of Pentecostal/charismatic worship are based on the emotions. If the worship service turned out to be a "good one," the Holy Spirit must have been present. However if one didn't "feel" right about worship, then perhaps the Holy Spirit was absent. Much of Pentecostal/charismatic worship and spirituality is grounded in this highly-subjective experiential mode.

However, while worship in the Orthodox Church is certainly experiential, incorporating all of our human senses, it is not based upon one's emotions, creative spontaneity, or the personality of the worship leader. Instead, it is based upon the time-honored and time-tested words and actions of the Apostolic Church.

I finally moved on from the Pentecostal/charismatic sector and fully embraced the historic Orthodox Faith. In the fall of 1990, I entered Saint Vladimir's Orthodox Seminary to pursue ordination to the priesthood in the Orthodox Church, and later was ordained to the diaconate and began to serve at Saint Mary's Orthodox Church in Brooklyn, New York. In early 1992 I was ordained to the priesthood.

I can honestly say that the Holy Orthodox Christian Faith has answered not only my basic questions, but it continues to answer each question that arises concerning my life in Christ and His Church.

But let me say something else. I owe much to Zion Bible College. It taught me to trust God and to search for the truth wherever it led me, and it instilled in me a great desire for the Apostolic Faith. I appreciate its emphasis upon the Holy Spirit, for it was the Holy Spirit that led me to the Orthodox Christian Church.

Although I doubt whether the faculty of Zion College would understand all of my reasons for leaving the Pentecostal movement to become Orthodox, I don't think a faculty member or student there would disagree with the words of one of the greatest Orthodox saints, Saint Seraphim of Sarov, who once told a seeker: "The true aim of our Christian life consists in the acquisition of the Holy Spirit of God."

Chapter Eleven

WHO SAYS
THE BIBLE SAYS?

By Fr. John Pro

With thirty-five years in the Baptist pastorate under my belt, I had learned how to field just about any question posed to me concerning the Scriptures or basic Christian theology. My years of teaching Sunday School and preaching from the pulpit had prepared me to respond to almost anything other people asked, no matter how unexpected or diverse.

Much harder to answer, however, were the quiet, nagging personal uncertainties which followed me throughout those years in the ministry. Although I seldom allowed myself to dwell on these uncertainties, I knew there were no pat answers or simple proof-texts for the internal theological dilemmas which often haunted me as I ministered to my Baptist parishioners.

The Question of Church

Perhaps the most difficult of these dilemmas centered around the subject of ecclesiology—the nature of the Church. In particular, I was troubled by the issue of Church government. My Baptist training had insisted upon the independence of every local Church, and the preeminence of the congregation as the final source of authority in all ecclesiastical matters. Similarly, training at other Protestant Christian schools (I hold a masters from the Pittsburgh-Xenia Seminary, a masters from Pittsburgh Theological Seminary, and a doctorate from Luther Rice Seminary) precluded a place for hierarchy in Church government.

A well-known Baptist training handbook states: "The government [of the Church] is administered by the body acting together, where no one possesses a preeminence, but all enjoy an equality of rights; and in deciding matters of opinion, the majority bears rule." This handbook goes on to say, "The pastor exercises only such control over the body as his official and personal influence may allow, as their teacher and leader and expounder of the great Lawgiver's enactments. His influence is paramount, but not his authority. In the decision of questions he has but his single vote" (Edward T. Hiscox, *The New Directory for Baptist Churches*, page 144).

Although I did my best to teach and practice such Baptist traditions, it was not easy to get around passages in the Scriptures which seemed to me to teach something quite different than the type of Church government described in that manual.

Particularly troubling for me at the time was Matthew 16:18 where the Lord Jesus Christ states to Peter, "I will build My Church and the gates of hades will not prevail against it." Starting at Pentecost, the Lord undertook that building process, using His

Spirit-empowered Apostles and their followers to do the job. Where was this strength of apostolic leadership today?

Of course even congregational Churches like the Baptists believe there are some church offices, such as pastors and deacons. These offices were, in some manner, in place in all the Christian groups of which I had been a part. Yet the continual splits, theological heresies, the proliferation of sub-denominations growing out of these Churches—despite the relatively short time they had been on the scene of Church history—bore witness that something was drastically wrong. Although those offices were in place, something had obviously broken down in terms of their manifestation to and through the Church.

In times of doubt and discouragement, it almost appeared that the gates of hell *had* prevailed against the Church, and that, in fact, hell had turned the tables and was now pressing out a relentless counter-assault. Of course I knew better than to entertain such thoughts, but at times it seemed as though the Church of Christ was in full retreat, divided, scattered, and in disarray.

Beware of Hebrews!

The issue of Church government finally came to a head as I was preparing a series of sermons on the Book of Hebrews. When I reached the thirteenth chapter, verses which I had read dozens of times before suddenly lunged out at me in vivid and unmistakable color.

"Remember your leaders, those who spoke to you the word of God; consider the outcome of their life and imitate their faith" (Hebrews 13:7 RSV).

"Obey your leaders and submit to them; for they are keeping watch over your souls, as men who will have to give account. Let them do this joyfully, and not sadly, for that would be of no advantage to you" (Hebrews 13:17 RSV).

Though I was already very familiar with this chapter, I began to see for the first time the reality of Church authority as it had been established by Christ Himself, and practiced by the Church throughout the ages. Not only had He established the four orders of the Church (bishops, pastors, deacons, and laity), He commanded His people to be in submission to those in authority in the Church, and to obey them in all things. In short, my study of Hebrews led me to the conclusion that a hierarchical Church government was the New Testament norm.

While the New Testament hierarchical structure does not ignore the importance of the congregation (the Church has always stressed the dignity and value of all four orders), it does reveal a system of decency and order in terms of how the Church is to operate. Christ promised the gates of hell would not prevail against the Church, because He Himself established the proper structure necessary to preserve and maintain her strength and unity throughout the centuries. Without that structure, and without a willing obedience by the people to those in authority, the true Church would not have survived.

I decided to preach a sermon on the theme "Scriptures Baptists Don't Like to Hear." In the introduction, I pointed out how we Baptists say with pride that we are "people of the Book" and "the New Testament is our rule of authority and practice." I said that "we pride ourselves on the doctrine of soul liberty and local Church autonomy." But I went on to point out that something was amiss here, since this passage in Hebrews doesn't seem to honor these long-standing Baptist traditions. We, as Baptists, don't believe there are any leaders put in charge of us by God, nor that we must submit to them and obey them. As I finished the sermon I asked the question, "Why do we ignore this rather plain passage of God's Word?"

There was much angry reaction. I was visited by deacons who said my sermon angered them and they wanted no more of this sort of thing. I was to retire in two months and was leaving on a month's vacation. When I returned I was not allowed to preach the remaining weeks till my retirement. I was paid off for my time remaining and was told not to return to the pulpit.

My experience in preaching through the Book of Hebrews, and the further research which followed, convinced me thoroughly that the Bible—Old Testament and New—taught a hierarchical form of government among God's people. Now a new problem presented itself. There is more than one group of Christians with a hierarchical structure to their ecclesiology. Which to choose?

Finding My Bishop

My first thought was to go to Roman Catholicism. I even applied for Holy Orders. At this point, God brought Father John Abdalah, an Orthodox priest at Saint George Orthodox Church in New Kensington, Pennsylvania, into my search. Father John challenged me to consider Orthodox Christianity. I was open. When he invited me to attend a liturgy at which some members of the Evangelical Orthodox Mission were to concelebrate, I was delighted to accept.

The liturgy was beautiful. Though I was not at all acquainted with Orthodox worship, I was nonetheless fascinated by the service and experienced a wonderful feeling of "at homeness." Further study and observation (for I began to attend services from that day on) revealed a scriptural relevance along with a delightful molding of Old and New Testament worship.

I needed no further convincing! I had found the Church

which our Lord said would stand the test of time and assault the very gates of hell. I asked for and received chrismation from the Right Reverend George Corry, priest at Saint Michael Church in Greensburg, Pennsylvania. Further delight came to me as my dear wife followed me into the Orthodox Church within two weeks. I withdrew my petition for Holy Orders in the Roman Church and wrote to Metropolitan PHILIP of the Antiochian Archdiocese to consider my desire to become a priest. My appetite for continued study was satiated as Father Abdalah kept supplying me with books to read. This, along with participation in the Divine Liturgy and other services of the Orthodox Church, served to sanction the leading of the Holy Spirit in my life.

I then enrolled in the Saint Stephen's Correspondence Course and finished it in a year. In the meantime I heard from Metropolitan PHILIP and passed the scrutiny of the ordination council and was ordained a deacon on February 28, 1988. I was assigned to Saint Michael Orthodox Church in Greensburg, Pennsylvania, with Father Corry. I invested time learning the rubrics and the chanting. In eight months Father Corry retired and I was then assigned to Father Abdalah in New Kensington, Pennsylvania, a short distance away. I continued to grow in understanding Orthodox worship.

In May, 1988, I was ordained to the priesthood by Bishop ANTOUN and continued to serve in New Kensington. Then in September, 1989, I was temporarily assigned as associate pastor of Saint George in Pittsburgh, Pennsylvania. Now I am once again serving the Lord in New Kensington.

What a joy Orthodoxy is! And what marvelous love has been shown to me by our bishops. They certainly have been used of God to fulfill my wish to continue to be an ordained servant of our Precious Saviour.

Some time ago I had the joy of watching a video tape of the entrance of the Evangelical Orthodox Church into canonical Orthodoxy. Metropolitan PHILIP made a statement at one point in the video: "Orthodoxy is the best kept secret in America." It certainly was for me. But, thanks to the leading of the Holy Spirit, he challenged me through the obedience of Father Abdalah. The secret has now been revealed to me and my family. Orthodoxy is no longer hidden. It is now the precious Faith which resides in our hearts.

Praise be to God for His grace!

Chapter Twelve

WHERE FOUNDATIONS WILL NOT CHANGE

By Fr. Athanasios Ledwich

M y particular odyssey to Orthodoxy began from Anglicanism in its Irish form—the Church of Ireland. My father was an Irish High Church clergyman—of a sort which used to be more common than it is today. He had a profound sense of reverence. His doctrine was impeccably sound, within High Church Anglican limits.

(The terms "High Church" and "Low Church" are popular ways of describing two quite separate traditions within Anglicanism. Sometimes the terms "Anglo-Catholic" and "Protestant" or "evangelical" are used. The High Church or Anglo-Catholic tradition was a force in the seventeenth century and was revived by the "Tractarians"—Newman, Pusey, and Keble—in the 1830's and '40's. This tradition emphasized the doctrine of the early Fathers, the sacraments, and beauty in worship, and restored monasticism in the Church of England.)

Despite the High Church emphasis of my father's parish, I remember a certain bareness about our worship, a lack of color, which is very characteristic of Irish Protestantism.

At the age of thirteen, I went to Saint Columba's College, near Dublin, the only British public school in the Republic of Ireland. Saint Columba's was founded in the 1840's by an English tractarian clergyman. When I was there, the only traces of this tradition were a simple but beautiful chapel and sung Anglican matins on Sunday mornings. All the boys wore white vestments, called surplices, as in an Oxford or Cambridge chapel. These services seemed to me the ultimate in ceremonial beauty.

Trinity College, Dublin

From Saint Columba's, I went on to study at Trinity College in Dublin. This gave me an opportunity to worship at Saint Bartholomew's, a well-known High Church center in Irish life. I can well remember the first moment I went into this Church. It had much in common with an Orthodox Church: it was dark, the walls were stenciled with iconographic paintings of the saints, and the chancel was dominated by an icon of Christ the Pantocrator.

When I first went in, I felt an overwhelming sense of holiness. The Church suggested the presence of God. A priest was heard but not seen reading week-day matins. If I had a moment of conversion to Orthodoxy in its true spirit, I would identify that moment in Saint Bartholomew's, Dublin.

During my years as an undergraduate I also came across

a book called *The Orthodox Church* by one Timothy Ware. I knew nothing about Orthodox Christianity, let alone the young Oxford academic layman who wrote it. I read the book from cover to cover and was totally transformed. I had no idea before then that the Christianity which had begun to take shape in my own mind could have such intellectual coherence, logical beauty, and ancient claims. I have read that book many times now, and have loaned or given more copies than I can remember to others.

Soon I became convinced the Orthodox Faith was true. So why did I not become Orthodox straight away? Primarily, I became painfully aware of how difficult such a step would be. My father, I thought, would have been deeply hurt by what he would have seen as my rejection of the Church of my upbring- ing. I supposed my mother would have also been pained (although twenty years later she became the first catechumen I received into Orthodoxy).

There were no Orthodox Churches in Ireland. And indeed I was scarcely aware of the depth of Orthodox worship. I had no Orthodox priest to guide me, and the one from whom I sought advice thought I had not explored the matter deeply enough. Naturally, the Anglican clergy whom I consulted tried to discourage me from going any further.

What was the result? I turned back.

Much that was attractive in Orthodoxy I felt could be realized in Anglo-Catholicism. I cannot imagine now twenty-five years later how different my life would have been had I become Orthodox then. I can only say that I acted in good faith, and I hope I will be able to defend that decision on the Day of Judgement. I do know that the experience of being an Anglican clergyman is something that has sharpened my awareness of Orthodoxy in all its truth. And though I have come to the Orthodox fold late,

I have come to it more strongly for the delay.

Life as an Anglican Priest

I decided to seek ordination as an Anglican clergyman. After my first degree I went to study theology at Durham University. In 1973 I was ordained in Manchester and went to work as a curate in an historic Lancashire mill town called Oldham. It was my first experience of what the Church of England can really be like away from the magic of an Anglo-Catholic parish. It was a "Town Center" Church, neither High nor Low. And it was totally dead!

I tried to live out a priestly life as I saw it, but was discouraged from doing so at every turn. Though there were three clergy on the staff, the other two did not believe that daily services were important. I well remember the sexton cleaning the chapel one day when I was about to celebrate a Eucharist. He looked at me with blank amazement. "Eh, lad, yar floggin' a dead 'orse," he said. Upset at the time, I realize now how right he was. I completed two unhappy years at Oldham and determined that for my second parish I would return to an Anglo-Catholic environment.

I found a good parish in another industrial town, this time in the Northeast of England. There was a splendid Anglo-Catholic priest there, who taught what we called "the full faith." We had a daily Mass, a sung Mass on Sunday, we heard confessions, we visited the people and tried to talk to them about God. I was completely happy in pastoral work there and spent three good years.

Serious Questions

The problem there arose not from the parish, but from the

Church at large. It was in 1976 that the infamous book *The Myth of God Incarnate* was published. The bishop of the diocese appointed a Canon Missioner who defended the book in an article in the diocesan magazine. My vicar and I were deeply shocked. We wrote a reply to the magazine, in which we pointed out that in defending the book, the Canon Missioner was denying the biblical stance of the Council of Chalcedon and the very heart of the Christian faith: that Jesus Christ is true God and true Man.

It seemed to me strange at the time that the Christian Faith should be a matter of opinion. Was it not the very foundation of all our teaching? I was even more shocked to discover the bishop denounced us at a meeting of the diocesan synod for having had the temerity to disagree with the standard Anglican line! Further shattering experiences were to come.

I knew I wanted to combine my priesthood with school mastering. So in 1978 I moved to Hereford where I was to be chaplain at the Cathedral School, to teach theology to youngsters between the ages of eleven and eighteen, and to be Vicar Choral at the Cathedral. Naively, I went hoping to influence at least the school's chapel life in an Anglo-Catholic direction. I went with the assumption I had since ordination and which seemed to me to be the only theological reason for being an Anglican, that the Church of England taught the full Orthodox Faith. Regrettably, I thought, certain people deviated from it; these people were not, however, truly Anglican.

With the blessing of my headmaster, I introduced a school patronal festival. Mary, the Mother of God, would be patron saint of the school and we would celebrate her on the Feast of the Annunciation. The result was a complete uproar! Canons of the Cathedral, parents of the school, the staff, and even the pupils thought that the Pope of Rome had taken over the school!

I realized with a jolt what I think many Anglo-Catholics never realize: catholicism in the Church of England works in isolated Anglo-Catholic shrines, but it is alien to Anglican teaching as a whole. For the vast bulk of Anglicans, whether laymen or clergy, many of the doctrines of Orthodoxy—the Mother of God, the saints, the sacraments—are all considered papal heresy.

Anglicans, however ecumenical they may be in our own time, look back to a Protestant foundation, articulated in the *Book of Common Prayer* and the *Thirty-Nine Articles*, both of which are profoundly Protestant. There is a more Orthodox element to Anglicanism indeed, but it has never established more than small and unpopular pockets of loyalty within the Anglican fold.

The Final Straw

Then came the Durham fiasco of 1984, details of which I have told in a book called *The Durham Affair* (Stylite Publishing Ltd., 1985). David Jenkins was a professor at Leeds University who was elected to the vacant See of Durham. Following his election he appeared on television denying the virgin birth and the bodily Resurrection of Christ as historical events. It seemed to some of us that we could not let such a radical statement pass without challenging the rightness of ordaining him to the episcopacy.

This seemed to me a test case. If the Church of England were to consecrate a man who had openly uttered such heresy in public without asking him to retract, then it was not a single bishop who was at fault: it was the whole body which made him a bishop that could be accused of heresy. It was a theological litmus paper which was certainly vital for me. After a petition to the Archbishop of York, the consecrating bishop, and a national furor which gripped the media for two months, the Archbishop decided he would proceed with the consecration. The Church of England after all, he said, was a comprehensive body which tolerated all manner of belief so long as the Creed could in good conscience be said.

Following the consecration I offered my resignation as a clergyman of the Hereford Diocese, and gave up my job as chaplain at the Anglican school.

The Orthodox Church

The following months were both decisive and re-invigorating. I spent two months traveling in Greece and Yugoslavia. I visited the ancient center of monasticism on Mount Athos. I spent three months reflecting and writing about my experiences. In December of that year I was received into the Orthodox Church by the now bishop, Kallistos Ware, in Oxford. It was an important climax of a journey to Orthodoxy which had started twenty years previously with the reading of Bishop Kallistos' book.

My story is one which can also be repeated by many, many fellow Anglican clergy who have moved either to Orthodoxy or to Rome. Many others I know hover on the brink. It is a story which, perhaps inevitably, focuses more on a negative experience than on a positive one. I regret this.

When I became Orthodox I plunged into a world and a Church which had in many ways been far at the back of my mind during the previous twenty years. It is difficult to appreciate the beauties of the harbor and its surrounding countryside when you are struggling to swim in a tempestuous storm at sea.

I have been Orthodox since the mid-1980's, and I have found immeasurable and unimaginable happiness. Of course we have problems in Orthodoxy. There are problems of jurisdiction, problems between ethnic Churches, and more.

However it remains true that even with the problems, in Orthodoxy there is the Faith, and it is a faith which is available to the experience of those who live it. It is a faith which brings joy and certainty. It is the Faith of the Fathers, the Faith of the Apostles, and the Faith given to us by Christ.

I can only stand in wonder and gratitude at the providence of God who brought me to this Faith, even though, through my own fault, I have come the hard way.

Chapter Thirteen

OUR SURPRISING SALVATION

By Fr. Harold Dunaway

I was born on the notable day of January 1, 1929, the year of the stock market crash, in Maysville, Kentucky, a small town on the Ohio River. There I grew up with a bunch of "river rats," or "rogues," from the East End of town. The East End was not exactly uptown, but my parents were simple folk and would have been delighted but uncomfortable living anywhere else. My father worked in a factory, when he could find work. During the Depression money and work were hard to come by. So when I was very young we moved in with other members of my father's family and lived on water-gravy, biscuits, and government commodities.

My parents were just nineteen years old when I was born. Both were very interested in following the Lord and in doing His will. Their Church was Pentecostal (Pilgrim Holiness—an off-shoot of the early Methodist Church), and despite their difficulties they were active and enthusiastic for a goodly number of years.

My father wanted very much to be a missionary to China. But for my mother it was too risky. Instead, in the style of most home folks, she wished to remain close to her mother, and so persuaded him to forget China. Later my father told me that he once took me into a Church and dedicated my life to the mission field in place of his own.

Life with Uncle Sam

At the ripe old age of sixteen, I decided to drop out of school, and Church, and join the Army. The road to glory then for us river boys was to become a soldier. Against my parents' wishes, I convinced an inebriated uncle to sign papers saying I was of legal age. A few months later and half-way across the Pacific I was discovered and discharged. So it was back to forking cans at the Carnation Milk factory for a while. Then the Korean conflict broke out and this time I made it to the real war—as a clerk typist. There in a tent in the dead of winter I soon began to lose the feeling of glamour and travel I had associated with military life.

Three years later, after reading Thomas Wolfe's *You Can't Go Home Again*, I headed home again—to say good-bye. On the way, I stopped in Albuquerque, New Mexico, to visit my sister. Driving down the main street of Albuquerque, I stopped at an insurance office to try for a job. I was hired and thus began the next phase of life, the "insurance industry."

Sales and Seeking

Two years later I met Barbara Ann Johnson and my life

has never been the same. Due to my sales ability (she states firmly), I took her by whirlwind. I proposed on our second date and urged her to agree to marry me four months later. Her family was Methodist, and her grandmother arranged our wedding and even a bout of pastoral counseling. It was the first time I had been in Church in twelve years.

Our son, Marc, was born nine months and one day after our wedding. Barb's spiritual life at this time was steadier than mine and even in our whirlwind courtship she had found words enough to ask about my relationship with God. I assured her I was "seeking," to get her off my back. The conversation went from there to other matters. I did, however, occasionally think about my relationship with God, which had flopped terribly after I rebelled against the Pentecostal God of my family. It was all "no this" and "no that," as far as I could see, a straight-laced, sober, and sad religion, and I favored my "funny-books" and "cornsilks behind the barn" to piety of the Pentecostal sort.

Soon Barb and I made friends with some neighbors in Albuquerque of the Baptist persuasion. They were quite evangelical by nature, and sought our friendship quickly. Between trips to the health spa and coffee in their home, Raymond shared his devoted faith in Christ with me. Mary, his wife, also entered heartily into these discussions and she enlisted Barbara to pray for me and for my salvation.

One afternoon Raymond and Mary decided to visit and either push me over the edge of my resistance, or give up completely. I showed my scorn for their "witnessing" (even though I liked them) by pulling out glasses of wine and piles of cigarettes, which I hoped would ward them—and God—off. My upbringing had convinced me that God was totally offended with such habits, and they were thus my weapons of defense. But to Raymond and

Mary they were no problem at all. *My soul melted* that day as Raymond handed his Bible to me and asked me to read from Romans 10:9: ". . .that if you confess with your mouth the Lord Jesus and believe in your heart that God has raised Him from the dead, you will be saved."

I began to read, and suddenly found myself on my knees before our couch with Raymond beside me. It was a moment to remember forever, and I shall. Unlike the normal conversion to Christ, it was an extremely dramatic moment for me. And I recall "floating" across the street to their house and joining them and other neighbors in praise and hymns.

Barb and I were both baptized soon after by their pastor at the Baptist Church. I was still on a cloud of disbelief at my belief. I continued to sell insurance, moving to Lubbock, Texas, where our second son, Michael, was born. I broke national selling records for the company, and trained several other men to do the same thing. It was high-flying time for my sales life, and I enjoyed it. And even though the travel robbed me somewhat of my family and Church, I loved to tell others about the Lord and my conversion. Often my salesmen would get a message about following God, as well as about how to sell.

Four years after our third child and first daughter, Luanne, was born we managed to transfer back to Kentucky. There we settled in a lovely rented home in the midst of a farm on the outskirts of Lexington. The only problem was that the Baptist Church was not the same without the people and pastor we first knew. I felt let down.

Go West!

This disappointment was relieved by meeting a young staff member from Campus Crusade for Christ, Jay Kulina. Jay and

I hit it off well. He had a new tool of evangelism, the "Four Spiritual Laws," and I had always had an immense desire to successfully "win someone to Christ." I had talked about Christ to many, but I had never "closed a sale," so to speak. Under Jay's spiritual guidance I became a freer and more fruitful Christian, and for the first time in my life I began to lead other men to Christ.

Before long I received and heeded the call to the ministry. Actually, the work of God was overtaking my insurance work. The men came to me to turn in their reports and stayed to talk about Christ. Our home became headquarters for discussing the Faith. So in 1966, at age thirty-seven, I enrolled at Bible Baptist College, in Springfield, Missouri. Our family had an all-out auction, sold nearly everything we owned, cashed in our company's retirement program, and headed west. After two years at BBC, I headed even further west to San Bernardino, California, to become part of the military division of Campus Crusade. Then, just two months later, in the fall of 1968, we were sent (of all places!) to Anchorage, Alaska.

We drove the long, unpaved Alaska Highway in early winter and arrived in Anchorage with seventeen dollars to our name. The next few years were spent learning to live moment-by-moment—depending on God for food, money, shelter, and words to say. I began to find men in the military who were eager to hear about Christ, and many responded to the presentation of the "Four Spiritual Laws" and to our teaching on the grace of God. Another group coming around our home was the "hippies" of the late '60's, who were also looking for something or someone to cling to. They, along with the young military men, began to accumulate in our living room. So I felt my next step was to leave Crusade staff, rather than being sent elsewhere, and continue discipling these new converts.

By God's grace we were able to purchase property in the nearby town of Eagle River in 1972. There were five acres on which stood a not-so-old, but neglected, Catholic convent. We moved in there, our family and nine single young adults, and from this place (now affectionately called the Big House) grew a Christian community. Three other men and I were ordained as "elders" of this new community in 1975. Many of my former Crusade associates came and helped teach us over the years, men such as Peter Gillquist, Jon Braun, Jack Sparks, Gordon Walker, and Richard Ballew.

The Final Phase

Little did I realize when I threw my hat into the ring with my old Crusade associates that my hat would become the hat of Orthodoxy. I had no inklings of going in that direction. All I wanted was to find and lead the people around me into the fullest expression of God's Kingdom possible. Just being a nominal sort of Christian would not suffice for us. We had a zeal for God, but still something seemed to be missing. What we needed to know was the fullness of the Faith.

We began to learn that Christianity was not just a me-and-Jesus religion. The Bible was clear that being a believer in Christ also had something (actually everything!) to do with a Kingdom. Investigating the Kingdom of God quickly led us smack into something called the Church. But what was this Church to be like? We felt it had to be more than we had experienced so far in our Christian life.

The men with whom I had joined ranks began to study early Church history. I had no inclination toward this kind of study myself, but I did have a chance to put into practice what they were discovering. They would learn something and we would immediately change and start doing it, whether it was calling for community, saying the Creed, making the sign of the cross, or worshipping with the Liturgy of Saint John Chrysostom. Church history soon gave us an appreciation for Orthodox Christianity, particularly the centuries around the great Church councils.

Finally, this search led us to seek union and communion with the Orthodox Church as it exists today. Make no mistake, though. This was *some* journey! It called for upheaval in nearly every aspect of my Christian belief. But all along there was that unmistakable ring of truth and a growing sense of satisfaction.

We were no longer running to the Christian bookstore to keep up with the hottest topic of the day. Instead, we were finding satisfaction in worship. There was difficulty to be sure. But there was also great excitement. And there were certainly times of despair and disillusionment (as, for example, when the Patriarch of Constantinople declined to see us, although the leaders of our denomination had travelled thousands of miles just to seek his direction). But there have also been times of inspiring vision and a glimpse of something so great it was worth selling all to obtain.

In September of 1986, Metropolitan PHILIP Saliba of the Antiochian Orthodox Church extended us a gracious invitation to enter his Archdiocese and we said thank you, we will! Our community in Eagle River, Alaska, was brought into the Church by Metropolitan PHILIP on April 1, 1987—a matchless day! By God's grace and with faith, our Church—now the Cathedral of Saint John the Evangelist—is committed to furthering the Orthodox Faith in modern Alaska and to continuing the work of our spiritual fathers.

My own life as a father in this Church has also evolved over a period of time. If I had my "druthers," I've told Barbara, I would choose to live out my days by the sea, close to the warm rays of

117

the sun, and bake in the sand. But we don't live as unto ourselves. I've had my days of doubts as to my qualifications as a priest of God (fortunately, some of the saints have had these same doubts!), and especially in the ancient Orthodox Church. But then I am reminded of the portion of Scripture that states, "No one, having put his hand to the plow, and looking back, is fit for the Kingdom of God" (Luke 9:62). It was He who chose me, after all.

Whatever it takes to attain the rewards of that Kingdom, I must do. And so I keep moving ahead in faith, repeating the constant prayer of all of us: Lord, have mercy.

Chapter Fourteen

SENT AWAY TO THE ANCIENT FAITH

By Fr. David Smith

There was no question which denomination I would serve when, in March of 1980, I decided to study for the pastorate. My family was United Methodist, all my Christian friends were United Methodists, and everything that had occurred in my life spiritually had taken place at the local United Methodist parish in suburban Syracuse, New York.

Through the ministry of our Methodist pastor, I had come to understand what it means to have Jesus Christ as Lord and Savior. I enjoyed growing up as part of a core group of youth at Church— and I experienced with them all of the spiritual exhilaration of retreats, Bible studies, social gatherings, and other youth functions.

When I announced my decision to enter the pastorate, my

relationship with the Church suddenly began to take on a new dimension. As people found out about my plans, I received more and more invitations to speak—I was asked to preach sermons, lead Bible studies, teach Sunday School classes, and I was given other leadership responsibilities.

The need arose for me to carve out my own identity as at least a *potential* spiritual authority. This meant learning how to do more than talk: I now had to find out if I really had anything to say! As a result, I started paying stricter attention to my prayer life and personal study of Scripture. I discovered I needed to do some careful thinking about my own faith.

Caught in the Middle

Concurrently, I found that the denomination at large was very different than my local congregation. When I spoke before certain other United Methodist groups about my zeal for the Church and for God, I encountered disbelief and indifference. I discovered a disdain for the supernatural at the denominationally-sponsored university I attended. Sometimes church authorities would emphasize professional matters, and ridicule my attention to spiritual development. I was being pulled in two opposite directions—spiritual versus institutional—as a result of my announced desire to become a pastor, and it was a very painful and confusing time.

Things came to a head in the summer of 1983. I maintained a friendly relationship with the pastor who supervised my candidacy, but we disagreed on almost everything about the Church and about Jesus Christ. One day, she said to me, "Why don't you consider another denomination? I don't think you'll be happy in the Methodist Church, and I don't think we'll be happy having you."

Strong statements from an inclusivist!

Her words hit me like a bolt of lightning. I had never supposed I would be anything besides Methodist. My first feeling was fear. It was like having my parents say to me, "We don't want you around anymore—why don't you look for another place to live?" Yet, I knew that she was right. I had sensed I would need to make this choice for some time, but never dared to put it into words. She casually sat across from me that day speaking the words I knew God wanted me to hear.

"Examine All Possibilities"

By the time I entered Asbury Theological Seminary in 1984, things had changed quite significantly in my life. I was now happily married. I had worked for two years as the director of an evangelical Christian camping center. And having left the Methodist Church, I was now attached to the Christian and Missionary Alliance. Deep down, I knew my questions concerning denominational issues had not all been settled. But with the rigors of a master of divinity program awaiting me, I knew some level of denominational sponsorship would be essential.

Seminary was a dream come true. We never had any money, we were always busy, and we never got enough sleep—but the fellowship and spiritual growth were staggering. Each day, as I returned from classes to our shabby little apartment, I thanked God for letting me live through this experience.

Something else impacted me in seminary—I got to know people from a large variety of denominations, all of them close to my own theological convictions. Soon after our arrival at Asbury I had decided I would "examine all possibilities" (as one of my Bible teachers often said), and choose the one denomination to which I could devote the rest of my life and energies.

At a time in life when I was doing the most searching, studying, and growing, this selection process appeared to be an ideal situation. I hadn't felt so confident and full of expectation since high school when a career exploration instructor proclaimed, "You can be anything you want to be!"

But somehow, I really couldn't decide. Everyone seemed to possess one small corner of the theological market, and each defended his claim fiercely—often, to the exclusion of other matters just as important. Seminary professors, thinking perhaps that the class before them was filled with denominationally secure people, readily pointed out the little inconsistencies in the various theological frameworks. I knew they were right! I had to think of some way that I could serve God as a pastor in an organization; not an organization that simply held beliefs closest to mine, but one which was sincerely closest to that of God's revelation through the Scriptures, and adhered to by His servants throughout the ages. Where would that be?

A Glimpse of Orthodoxy

I thought for some time about opening up my own Church and building Christianity from the ground up. Several questions bothered me. What will we do there? If all we do is sing, pray, and preach, why not go to the Assemblies of God down the street? If I practice another ritual besides this, what will it be? Am I just searching for something different in order to attract attention, or am I really seeking the truth? These questions bound me to the extent that fortunately I had to abandon my plans to open or serve in an independent Church.

Later, in a class on inner-city Churches, we visited various cities to do field work. I looked at many Churches. None were as interesting (and certainly none more unique!) as an Evangelical Orthodox Church (EOC) I encountered along the way. Here were a group of committed, biblical, evangelical Christians on their way to Orthodoxy. I only had a brief contact with the Church during October of 1985, but the impression of that visit, and the journey upon which the EOC had embarked, stayed with me. What an exciting perspective! In order to discover the real meaning of New Testament Christianity, they studied the Church that was born in the New Testament, and where it went in history!

Ups and Downs

For the rest of my seminary career, I felt like a closet Orthodox. When I wrote papers, I tried to discuss matters pertaining to Orthodoxy. When I studied Scripture, I wrestled with my concerns over Orthodox theology. I still remember one term paper on I Corinthians 11:23-26—the Eucharistic passage. As I translated, studied, and wrote, it seemed like God lifted a veil from my eyes concerning my long-held reductionist attitudes and beliefs concerning the Eucharist. I alternately experienced waves of joy and fear to think of what the "Body and Blood" actually meant for Christians.

But one significant negative experience also stands out in my mind. After some time of studying about Orthodoxy, my wife and I decided it was time to actually attend a service together. We often drove by an Orthodox Church on the way to work, so one Friday we stopped to attend services. A young man met us on the doorstep and told us a service was just ending, but that there would be another one tomorrow because it was the day before Easter.

As we drove away, we decided to go—but we also felt sorry for this poor soul who didn't seem to realize that Easter had already been celebrated that year! When we attended the next day, the experience was confusing and disappointing. We heard very little English, except when the priest yelled at the chanter or the people. Everyone came in late and tried to leave early. Few people said hello. Was this representative?

Later the next week, as I sat in the library at Asbury, I looked next to me on the magazine rack and saw a publication I'd seen at the EOC Church I had visited—*AGAIN* Magazine. Still smarting from our discouraging experience on Saturday, my wife was annoyed when I brought it home proclaiming there was still hope! Some months later, when another issue arrived at the seminary, I decided to take the plunge, and wrote to the managing editor, Deacon Ray Zell. He responded very quickly to tell me Father Gordon Walker was just one state to the south, Tennessee, and suggested I go to see him.

Nashville, Tennessee, may seem close to Lexington, Kentucky, to someone from the West Coast—but for a couple who had been disappointed by one Orthodox Church already, the four-hour drive seemed unreasonable! Several more months went by before the Holy Spirit's prompting was just too strong. Finally, my wife and I went to spend a weekend at Saint Ignatius Church in Franklin, Tennessee.

How can I describe that first liturgy—that is, the first liturgy I heard in English and could understand? Honestly, it was like reliving Saint John's revelations on Patmos. This time I wasn't just reading these revelations—I was experiencing them. As I looked over at my wife, I saw that she had the same response. When the people lined up to receive the Eucharist, I felt an attraction that nearly overwhelmed me.

If that day was our Orthodox birth, it was quickly followed by the growing pains of adolescence. I graduated from seminary with a masters of divinity—the most pointless degree in the world for anyone besides a pastor—and no Church to use it in. Instead, I found myself working in homeless services in Central New York while starting from scratch to learn the practices of Orthodoxy under Father Hannah Sakkab at Saint Elias Church in Syracuse.

There were so many lessons. Some of them didn't come easy to this young Asbury grad who had only recently learned of the existence of Orthodox Christianity. No matter how difficult some of those lessons were, though, I've never once looked back. I have an unchanging Faith I want to give to my children. I'm praying wise and ancient words. I'm worshiping God.

The New Beginning

I came home from a vacation in July, 1991 to a message on my answering machine from Bishop ANTOUN of the Antiochian Archdiocese of North America—I was to be ordained to the priesthood to serve the Holy Transfiguration Mission in London, Ontario. What a great new beginning it was!

Each week, I can't believe that I'm actually called to touch the Body of Christ with my own fingers, and to pray the words that the first Christians used—it's too good to be true, but I suppose grace always is.

My studies at Asbury Theological Seminary gave me the tools that I needed to authentically discover God's truth, and I continue to use them for the furtherance of His Kingdom. I still thank God that He called me to Asbury, for without doubt, that was the vehicle He chose to lead me to the wonderful joy and fulfillment I've now found in the Orthodox Faith.

Chapter Fifteen

ORTHODOXY COMES TO WHEATON

By Fr. Bill Caldaroni

My world seemed to be falling apart!

I had been raised in a mainline Protestant denomination, and for as long as I could remember felt called to the pastorate. As an adolescent my entire identity was built around that sense of pastoral calling. My family, the people of my home Church, and all my friends took it for granted that Bill Caldaroni was going to be a pastor in the United Church of Christ.

But now everything was topsy-turvy! Here I was in my second year of seminary, and I found myself questioning all the basic assumptions of my Protestant upbringing. I had confronted Orthodox Christianity and deep down inside knew all my well-laid career plans were going to be shattered. But let me back up a bit.

My Commitment to Christ

The United Church of Christ is a denomination which in the Sixties majored largely on issues of social justice and liberal theology. Although I felt I wanted to be a pastor in the UCC, Church life left a void in my heart. Social action was great, but something foundational seemed to be lacking.

I discovered what that "something" was in my early high-school years: a personal relationship with Jesus Christ. The ministry of Billy Graham—his biblical preaching and clarion call for total commitment to Jesus as Lord and Savior—captured me. I followed his exhortations to read the Bible, and its words seemed to resonate with life. I began to pray consistently, and I sensed the Lord's presence and forgiveness.

Often I would experience deep joy simply at repeating the name of Jesus over and over again. I had discovered the spiritual power of Jesus' name, something I have rediscovered years later in the "Jesus Prayer" of Holy Orthodoxy: *Lord Jesus Christ, Son of God, have mercy on me, a sinner.*

I began to read books on Scripture and theology. Now I felt I had a clearer sense of calling to the pastorate than ever before. I would enter the ministry of the UCC in order to be a reformer. I would be a voice calling for evangelism and a return to biblical roots.

I began to pursue my dream. I wanted to tell others about Christ. My pastor, a gentle and wise man, took me under his wing as a teenager and allowed me to teach a Bible study and to preach regularly. How thankful I am to him and to those people of my home congregation in Cleveland.

I must have grated on many people's nerves, however, with my youthful attempts to get them to see the necessity of making an overt, personal commitment to Christ. These were the days of the "Jesus Movement." All during high school I wore a "One Way" button, referring to Jesus as the one way to the Father (John 14:6).

A few of my high-school teachers decided they were going to challenge this young enthusiast so they began to make attacks on the intellectual integrity of Christianity. Unfortunately, some of their weapons hit the mark. I began to have doubts. I went through a period of about two years in which I was plagued with questions as basic as, "Is there a God? If so, is Jesus God? How do I know the Bible is true?"

I knew I had met God at those Billy Graham crusades, but the nagging doubts would not leave me. Thankfully, evangelical authors like F. F. Bruce, Clark Pinnock, and others helped introduce me to the good, solid apologetic grounds for Christian faith beyond the assurance of my personal experience.

Enough for secular education! I determined to go on to a Christian college which stood for a clear commitment to Christ and to the truth of my kind of Christianity. One day I caught a TV special with Oral Roberts in which he described the university he had built in Tulsa, Oklahoma. Intrigued, I sent for information. When it arrived, the literature from ORU sold me completely.

Those undergraduate years at ORU were the best four of my life so far. The school emphasized Christian discipleship and the necessity of obedience to Christ, wherever He may lead. There I had my first taste of Christian community in which we were taught to see each other as brothers and sisters in Christ and to use our spiritual gifts for building up the Body of Christ.

ORU taught me the necessity of being filled with the Holy Spirit. The "charismatic" emphasis was something foreign to me since I was basically an evangelical Protestant rationalist. But at ORU I discovered God to be bigger than my puny little intellect—

a lesson which opened me up to Holy Orthodoxy with its grand pursuit of the uncontainable God.

Above all, ORU taught me the splendor of Spirit-filled liturgical worship. The campus chaplain at that time was Reverend Bob Stamps, a charismatic Methodist minister. "Brother Bob," as we called him, shaped me more for Orthodoxy than I could ever have known at the time. Every Sunday evening a large group of students and people from the Tulsa Christian community would gather for a glorious service of worship called "Vespers." There was singing, praying, Scripture reading, and the high point of it all—the celebration of Communion. Only later did I discover that Bob Stamps had been engaged in a study of the ancient Church and its worship!

ORU set me up for Orthodoxy!

Seminary Years

I had planned for several years to attend seminary in the Chicago area at Trinity Evangelical Divinity School because of its strong commitment to biblical authority. The United Church of Christ officials at home approved of my choice somewhat reluctantly, but consented nonetheless. So after graduation from ORU, I went to Trinity—but not before meeting Janila Tilde Denison and falling deeply in love. Tilde was two years behind me in school, so while I moved to the Chicago area she remained at ORU in Tulsa. Our developing relationship continued by mail, phone, and visits.

By the end of the first year of seminary at Trinity, I began laying plans to return to ORU—this time to the seminary—for my second year. I wanted to be nearer to Tilde since we were considering the possibility of marriage. That second year proved to be decisive. After the first semester back, Tilde and I married.

However, that spring semester after our wedding proved to be one of the most challenging times of our lives.

I had enrolled in a course called "Eastern Christianity," taught by Dr. Theodore Williams, who was also a deacon in a local Orthodox Church. He was a strong advocate of Orthodoxy, and soon I found myself in the turmoil which I described as I began my story. Dr. Williams continually referred to the Fathers of the early Church and to the tradition of the Seven Ecumenical Councils.

In Church history courses at Trinity we had quickly glossed over those early years of the Church's history, so I decided to learn more about them. Dr. Williams challenged us to come to grips with the facts of tradition, sacrament, liturgical worship, veneration of the saints, and above all, the unbroken continuity of the Orthodox Church.

I determined to disprove the reality of Dr. Williams' claims. After all, my dreams to enter the Protestant pastorate were being challenged. Instead, however, my research proved the accuracy of his teachings. It was all there, just as he had stated! The Orthodox Church certainly seemed to be the fullness of the Christian Church.

But rather than making any sudden move, I spent the following year pastoring a rural circuit of evangelical Churches in Maryland. What a good year! It confirmed both my calling to the ministry and, through prayer and reading, my conviction of the truth of Orthodoxy. Also during this year I discovered an excellent book by Peter Gillquist, *The Physical Side of Being Spiritual* (Zondervan). This book summed up exactly what I had discovered to be the truth of Orthodoxy.

After corresponding with Peter Gillquist, Tilde and I began to plan to return to the Chicago area and Trinity Evangelical

Divinity School. And we hoped to learn more of the group with which he served, the Evangelical Orthodox Church (EOC).

Back in the Chicago area, we began attending the closest Evangelical Orthodox community, in nearby Gary, Indiana, pastored by Gregory Rogers. God's call seemed clear. These people of the EOC were on their way to Orthodoxy, and we desired to go along with them! My plans of a career as a full-time pastor seemed on indefinite hold, and my family back in Ohio (all of whom became Orthodox in 1990) questioned the wisdom of my move. But God's leading was apparent to Tilde and me.

Our Move into Orthodoxy

Upon finishing my master of divinity at Trinity we moved to Gary and spent the next six years, along with the rest of the brethren, on the long trek to Orthodoxy. During that period I worked as a home-electronics salesman. Finally in March of 1987, our EOC parish was brought into the Orthodox Church in the Antiochian Archdiocese. What a glorious day. The next day I, along with several other brethren, received ordination as a priest in the Holy Orthodox Church. I was home!

Not long after that we began Holy Transfiguration Orthodox Mission near Wheaton College under the guidance and inspiration of Father Peter Gillquist. Having started from scratch, I am today the full-time priest of the mission, we have our own building, and we are growing a vital Orthodox community. Our parish includes people from all walks of life—from adult converts to students at Wheaton College. We are providing a much-needed Orthodox witness in this area often referred to as the "Vatican of Evangelicalism."

Evangelical Protestantism led me to Christ and nurtured me in discipleship. Without that blessed foundation I would never have been receptive to the riches of Holy Orthodoxy. Now we want to call the rest of our evangelical brethren—and all of America—home to the Orthodox Church. For it is here that we find the fullness of Christ. It is a great joy for me to lead others into the rich evangelical life of the Holy Orthodox Church!

Chapter Sixteen

FROM BIOLA
TO THE BARRIO

By Ron Olson

T he story of my journey to Orthodoxy is the very story of my life. Under God's sovereign hand I have experienced a converging effect, funneling me, as it were, towards the Orthodox Faith. All that preceded—my missionary work in South America and subsequent ministry to the inner-city poor, the people I have met, my training, even my artistic endeavors—have in some way pointed me "home."

My Protestant schooling played a major role in preparing me for a ministry within the Orthodox Church. This education did not begin with my training at Biola College in Los Angeles, California. In fact, I was in the "cradle roll" from the earliest weeks of my life at the Church of the Open Door in Los Angeles. Practically from infancy on, I began hearing Sunday school lessons, memorizing scripture verses, and spending several weeks per year at camps at Vacation Bible Schools.

You might say my evangelical Protestant credentials were impeccable. I even sat under the expository preaching of the renowned Bible teacher, Dr. J. Vernon McGee. Later, our family moved and began attending a Church led by another biblical expositor from Dallas Seminary. There I was baptized, had my first struggles with my faith, and met the young lady who would become my wife.

Unanswered Questions

At the age of thirteen I read the Gospels several times, prompted by a desire to really know Christ. Especially impressed by the Sermon on the Mount, I went to someone I respected and trusted to seek counsel on how, if possible, one could obey Christ's words in this sermon.

The response he gave was baffling: "Don't worry about those things. They're not for today. They're for a different dispensation." Even though I was barely a teenager, I knew I could never buy into any system of scriptural interpretation which rejected the clear teaching of Christ in this way. I stubbornly committed myself to the Christ revealed in the Gospel, hoping someday to be able to know how to obey Him.

Not many years later I set off for Biola College, hoping to prepare for Christian service, and at the same time find answers to the questions which had followed me throughout my Christian life. I sincerely wanted to serve God with my whole being, but as I left home my heart and mind were burdened with discrepancies between what the Bible seemed to be teaching, and the Christianity I had been practicing.

At Biola, some of those questions were clarified. The answers to others, however, were more obscure. I asked, "How can anyone know for sure his interpretation of the Bible is correct over against the interpretation of someone else?" "Why are certain things in Scripture supposed to be interpreted *literally*, but others *figuratively*—and more importantly, who is to decide?"

At times it almost appeared to me that anything in Scripture disagreeing with our Protestant belief system or middle-class American way of life was either ignored or else explained away. For instance, little was ever said about Matthew 25, where our Lord connects our salvation with what we do for Him in relation to the poor and the prisoner. We were taught the theology of Ephesians 2:8,9 ("For by grace you have been saved through faith, and that not of yourselves; it is the gift of God, not of works, lest anyone should boast") but not of verse 10 ("For we are His workmanship; created in Christ Jesus *for good works*, which God prepared beforehand" italics mine).

Doing good had no place in our doctrine.

Missionary Assignment

After a few years at Biola I ran out of money, moved in with some friends, and got a job. Later, I was married. Through striking circumstances and a clear moving in our hearts, God led my wife and me to the mission field in Colombia, South America. There we wrestled daily with the abject poverty around us, and the profound feeling we should be doing more. But what? Also, we studied the Scriptures more deeply and more passionately than before, for it was now *our turn* to pass on the Faith and respond to the challenges of the sects.

One day in Colombia a Jehovah's Witness pastor came to my door. Not wanting to waste time, I immediately told him Christ is God Incarnate. He contradicted me showing his proof-texts from the Bible. I tried to correct him, but with basically the same technique he was using. We continued in the same vein until he ended the conversation by insulting me and leaving. I had no doubt I was correct, but I still was left with a profound disquiet. Both of us claimed to hold the Bible as the final authority. Who was to be the referee?

We reluctantly returned to the United States after four years in Colombia, permanently changed by our experiences there. We would never be able to feel quite as comfy and cozy in our own affluent culture as we had before. For a few months, we searched for God's next step for us. Soon, we found ourselves working with a group called INNERCHANGE, seeking to identify with the poor Cambodian and Hispanic refugees in the inner city, bringing help, encouragement, and Christ to them as best we could.

This experience further alienated me from my evangelical roots. It was a move from a "positional righteousness" to a more biblical, "active righteousness." Simultaneous interest in the disciplines of fasting and prayer opened me tremendously to Orthodoxy when it was presented to me through the video *Welcome Home* and the book *Becoming Orthodox*. Filled with excitement at our "new discovery," Laurie and I spent the better part of a year studying and reading to each other in every spare moment, at home or in the car, researching the claims of Orthodox Christianity from many sources and perspectives. We found that even Orthodoxy's critics often corroborated its most important claims.

The Answer is Sometimes "Mystery"

What is more, my questions were at last being answered. As opposed to rationalistic Western theology, Orthodoxy leaves room for the unknown and teaches it is okay to look upon God as a mystery. God could no longer merely be systematized, analyzed, and synthesized at will. Prayer became more than rehearsing a laundry-list of petitions, or stubbornly trying to change God's mind. In Orthodoxy, prayer is perceived as a matter of turning our minds, hearts, and even our bodies toward the Triune God.

"Jesus *is* the answer" as we had so often taught, but union with Christ is a moment-by-moment process to be experienced as a whole human being: soul, spirit, and body. Such a union is the ultimate answer to everything. The Church teaches Christ *is* present in the poor for those who would love Him there. What a relief!

At present, my wife and I are beginning an Orthodox work with the inner-city poor, under the direction of Father Jack Sparks, focusing, at least for now, on Hispanics. We live in Santa Ana, California, in an all-Hispanic barrio. Our desire is to bring Christ and His Church to the poor in a way that will reproduce itself many times over and meet the needs of the immediate communities around us. We are still struggling to gain the financial freedom to devote ourselves full time to this work, but are encouraged by all the opportunities for service which lie ahead.

For me, Orthodox Christianity is the fulfillment of my faith in Christ: it is as the truth should be. Finding it feels both like coming home and beginning a journey. We're grateful beyond words that God has brought us here.

Chapter Seventeen

IN THE BREAKING OF THE BREAD

By Tim Blumentritt

As we gathered every Lord's Day morning for the breaking of bread, our thoughts were focused on the worship that was taking place in heaven before the throne of God. Our hymns were often filled with the imagery of the heavenly temple described in Hebrews. Yet, our experience of heaven had no physical manifestation. The walls of our modest meeting rooms and halls were unadorned by art or symbols, and even the cross was noticeably absent from our building and our persons.

Brethren conducted the quiet and orderly service, and sisters with veiled heads participated silently. Although we claimed to disdain prescribed liturgy, our worship invariably began with extemporaneous prayers, *a cappella* hymns, and scripture readings, and culminated in the Lord's Supper. A loaf of leavened bread and a common cup of wine were blessed and shared among those within the fellowship. Like the early Church, visitors and inquirers could observe, but not participate. Though the bread and wine were symbolic, we believed Christ was really present in our gathering. Worship was the center of Church life.

Despite a common bond with hundreds of similar gatherings, church government was strictly congregational with no central organization, headquarters, or hierarchy. We rejected both the ordination of clergy and Protestant denominationalism as incompatible with the nature of the Church and accepted no title other than the description "Christians Gathered to the Name of the Lord Jesus"—others called us the Plymouth Brethren.

Growing Up Among the Brethren

I was raised by devout parents in a small, closely-knit Brethren community. Even when very young, my goal was to join the group of itinerant evangelists and teachers which circulated among our congregations. Though I had sometimes practiced my evangelism on unsuspecting passersby, only after my own requisite crisis conversion experience and baptism at age fourteen was I able to actively pursue preparation for the ministry.

Soon after its beginnings, the Brethren movement had succumbed to a rigid sectarianism based on principles of church organization. In later years, both scholarship and spiritual life suffered greatly under the influence of fundamentalist ethics and anti-intellectual bias. Seminary education was regarded as a temptation to compromise our principles and was deeply suspect, but on-the-job training was encouraged.

I worked two summers with tent-meeting evangelists in the Midwest and graduated from high school a year early at age seventeen to pursue this activity full time. My mentors wisely suggested that education and employment would help provide the maturity for such work, so I enrolled in college and found a job.

Rocking the Boat

During college, I spent six months in Britain and Ireland among some of the original Brethren communities. Noting the diversity even within the Brethren movement challenged my provincial outlook. With ecclesiastical roots extending only to the 1830's, our claim to be the heirs of the Apostolic communities seemed tenuous at best. The Brethren subscribed to the typical evangelical view of Church history with vague references to the apostasy of the early Church and the Dark Ages of Catholicism. We lauded the efforts of the reformers, but recognized the full maturity of the Church only in the evangelical missionary movements of the nineteenth century, and in the development of dispensationalism by J. N. Darby, a scholarly Anglican cleric, who became a prominent leader among the early Brethren.

More disturbing, however, was the Brethren's claim to be successors to a long line of separatist dissent from the established Church. Our revisionist history defended some aspects of early heretical movements—especially Montanism and iconoclasm.

At work I became, for the first time, close friends with a Christian from a liturgical Church. Having been baptized Lutheran as an infant, Mary met none of my criteria for being "saved" and I did my best to remedy the situation. Ultimately, her sincere commitment to Christ forced me to question my own rigid categories and naive assumptions about salvation and the spiritual life.

God's Kingdom, Now

As I became more responsible for evangelism and teaching, I realized that the "gospel" we preached came almost exclusively from Saint Paul's epistles. Jesus' teachings did not fit so neatly into categories of man's total depravity, salvation by faith alone, crisis conversion experiences, and the eternal security of the believer. Jesus announced the Kingdom of God and called not only for repentance but perseverance. I attempted to preach the same message and was sharply corrected for having confused the gospel of the Kingdom, which was addressed to the Jews, with the gospel of grace, as taught by Saint Paul.

Though still a dispensationalist, I gradually became increasingly aware that the eternal Kingdom of God was the principal theme of the entire Scripture and was not simply limited to "the Millennium." The dissection of texts into parts addressed to the Jews and parts to the Church seemed increasingly artificial as I discovered, even at the close of Acts, the Kingdom being boldly preached by Saint Paul. In the Book of Revelation, the Kingdom is found everywhere as the theme of the hymns of praise and worship before God's throne.

Covenant theology helped me to reassemble the truths which dispensationalism had fragmented. I discovered the unity between the Two Covenants: the New Covenant *fulfilled* the Old. I saw that the Church could not be divided from the Kingdom which was both "now" and "not yet." What a relief to discard dispensationalism's strained exegesis and elaborate charts diagraming the details of future events!

The Kingdom of God filled my thoughts, my teaching, and my public prayers during worship. The elders were baffled by my fascination with what they considered to be part of another dispensation—the Jewish Millennium. My fading commitment to dispensationalism had been viewed with deep suspicion and distaste, but when I disclaimed the integral doctrine of the secret rapture of the Church, their toleration ended. I was not asked to preach anymore, and respected preachers told me privately that I had no future among them if I continued to embrace "false" doctrine.

At this, I quietly and reluctantly began my search for a Church where such doctrine was welcome. Seminary education to prepare for ministry or teaching in an academic environment was now a possibility. After contact with some of the faculty of Reformed Theological Seminary (particularly one who was raised among the Plymouth Brethren), I made plans to attend.

Though I had already perceived that worship was to be a celebration of the Kingdom, I knew no way in which this could be expressed other than the extemporaneous prayers of Brethren worship. I had never attended the worship service of another Church. Visiting other Churches was strongly discouraged, and my empty seat in our small gathering would draw immediate attention.

Deeply impressed with Reformed theology, I visited several Churches of that tradition expecting a joyful celebration of the presence of the Kingdom. I was terribly disappointed—a few hymns and prayers before a long sermon fell far short of the worship revealed in the Scriptures. Though I was accustomed to the Lord's Supper every Sunday, I could not yet explain why these cerebral worship services with no Communion seemed especially empty.

Narrowing the Options

I soon found the explanation in Robert Webber's *Evangelicals on the Canterbury Trail*. He introduced liturgy and sacrament as the way to experience the presence of the Kingdom in worship. My girlfriend, later my wife, Carol, also read the book and we were both moved by the stories of evangelicals attracted to the liturgical Church. We seemed to be on the same journey, yet with little clue as to our destination.

Seeking an experience similar to one described in the book, I inquired at local Episcopal Churches. Though none admitted to being the "High Church" for which I was searching, one said, "Oh, we drag out the incense every now and then!" Nevertheless, we attended on Christmas Eve and were immediately attracted to the beauty and the content of the liturgy.

Webber made the Episcopal Church sound appealing, but the doctrinal upheaval and moral confusion which it had suffered along with other mainline Protestant Churches distressed us. I had been in England and had followed in the press the consecration of the infamous Bishop of Durham. I was amazed that such leaders were tolerated in the Church—I knew nothing of Bishop Spong.

Though our bitterly anti-Catholic upbringing constrained us to remain this side of the Reformation, our honest search led us to attend Mass several times at a vibrant, charismatic Catholic parish. Spiritual life and enthusiasm were certainly evident, but my doctrinal questions went unanswered at the inquirer's class. We had reached an impasse in that we could not envisage being either Roman Catholic or Episcopalian, yet we knew no other option.

Orthodox Ups and Downs

Curious about Webber's references to Orthodoxy, I drove past the nearest Church. The Church's building was large and beautiful, but there wasn't any notice board listing times of services, and my phone calls were unanswered—it seemed they were not expecting visitors. Nevertheless, I hesitantly walked in one Sunday morning carrying my Bible—I needn't have bothered. The service seemed to consist of a great deal of wailing from a podium in front, and a confused and feeble old priest occasionally emerging from behind a curtain to murmur something in a foreign tongue. There were no interpreters!

By the end of the liturgy, the congregation of five had grown to about thirty. Seemingly oblivious to the service, each newcomer had strolled to the front to light candles, greeting and conversing with others along the way. After the service, I was quizzed about my ethnic background. Though the building could have held 300, one parishioner confided to me that the crowd was larger than usual that day, since it was Orthodox Christmas. I was less than impressed. Later, I announced to Carol, "I visited the Orthodox today. There's no need to check them out any further."

Two weeks later, the newspaper's Religion section carried an interview with Father Peter Gillquist. He told about a group of evangelicals who were attracted to the liturgical, sacramental Church and had joined the Orthodox. The article also announced that Father Jon Braun would be speaking at a local parish, and the public was invited to hear him.

We went to the meeting that night and were not confronted with a confused and feeble old priest murmuring in a foreign tongue! I was fascinated with the story of the EOC's search for the New Testament Church, especially when Father Braun told me later they had investigated the Plymouth Brethren along the way.

Father Braun's conviction was contagious, and his advice the best. "The Orthodox Church *is* the Church of the New Testament," he told me, "and I'd recommend reading *For the Life of the World* by Alexander Schmemann." I later read all of Father Schmemann's books several times, and as much of the Saint Vladimir's Press list as I could acquire. More than anything else, God used Father Schmemann's writings to lead us to the Church.

After being assured the liturgy would be in English, I was in Church the following Sunday. What a thrill to hear for the first time, "Blessed is the Kingdom... now and ever and unto ages of ages."

Though I fell immediately in love with the liturgy, I cannot pretend that our transition into the Orthodox Church was easy. We were not looking for the perfect Church, yet the large, secularized, ethnic parishes seemed devoid of the spiritual vitality for which we were searching.

A Step of Faith

One by one, though, we discovered cradle Orthodox who confidently shared their faith with us. We were greatly encouraged by a visit to Saint Athanasius Church in Santa Barbara, California, where we met spiritually-alive Orthodox Christians who really understood our background and encouraged us to enter the Church. Father Jack Sparks challenged me: "You can't wait until you learn everything about it, you have to take this as a step of faith."

After reading all the Orthodox literature I could find, and having gained an appreciation for its theology and liturgy, I was still apprehensive about embracing the Church in its present form. Father Thomas Hopko, a prominent lecturer and professor at Saint Vladimir's Seminary in New York, insisted, however, that despite the effects of history, politics, and ethnicism on the Church, it was yet the only Church which did not require me to believe anything untrue.

I realized that this basic dogmatic position was unavoidable. Though some doctrines and practices still confused me, I finally admitted that even if I were able to acquire perfect knowledge of all the ways in which the Church had developed throughout history, I would still be incapable of deciding whether it had gone wrong or right. I understood then that Father Sparks was correct: If the Church of the New Testament still existed, I would have to accept it by faith. I could not turn away saying, "Yes, it's the true Church, but it's too ethnic, or too difficult."

The Fullness of the Kingdom

After eighteen months of study, prayer, and conflicting emotions, my wife and I were chrismated and received into the Orthodox Church. Our decision to leave the Brethren seemed to them a kind of apostasy. Our families were disrupted and we lost a lifetime of relationships which had been built around the church fellowship. Though our families try to be loving and accepting, they are utterly bewildered by our beliefs. As with many evangelicals, the little they know of Orthodoxy appears not only incorrect, but distasteful or even shameful.

Our journey has taken us far from our roots, yet many aspects of our Brethren background shaped and prepared us for our new home. The centrality of heavenly worship and the Lord's Supper stirred within us the desire for a sacramental lifestyle centered around the Eucharistic Table. Even the deprivation of dispensational theology produced a hunger for the fullness of the Kingdom expressed here and now.

Although my understanding of what it means to be a leader and a teacher in the Church has undergone a drastic change since my youthful wish to be an itinerant preacher, the desire to serve

God has remained constant. I have been active in our new parish teaching Christian education and leading Bible studies for both adults and teens. In the future, I plan, God willing, to attend Saint Vladimir's Seminary to prepare further for a life of service in the Church—the Kingdom of God on earth.

Chapter Eighteen

AN ANGLICAN–ORTHODOX PILGRIMAGE

By Fr. William B. Olnhausen

G od works in mysterious ways.

In the 1950's my cousin married a Greek girl. We visited her family on Orthodox Easter, and at age fifteen I experienced feta cheese, ouzo, and just a taste of Pascha. I knew nothing of the Orthodox Church, but from that day on I had a warm spot in my heart (and stomach!) for Orthodoxy.

My religious experiences had run the gamut. My mother was Methodist, my father a lapsed Roman Catholic. We attended a revivalist Church in rural Ohio. Perhaps I wasn't paying attention, but religion there seemed to consist of just praising the Lord, no explanations given. I don't think I ever took it seriously. Now and then I went to Mass with my grandmother and was fascinated but didn't understand. I went to college and dropped out of religion.

It was late in my college experience that God began to move in my life. To everyone's amazement—including my own—I felt called to the ministry. I turned to mainline Protestantism, attracted by the kind of religion that wasn't afraid of honest thinking. I went to a liberal Methodist seminary and was quickly *overwhelmed* by honest thinking. "Don't accept anything on authority," we were told; "decide it for yourself." So I did. I decided theological issues were so complex that I needed authority. Who was I to invent or even re-invent the Christian religion? I needed someone or something higher and wiser than I.

With the help of a wise British Methodist professor, I decided I would simply believe what the vast majority of Christians had always believed. From that moment, though I didn't know it, I was becoming Orthodox at heart. For the first time, I accepted the Incarnation of the Son of God. Shortly thereafter, in an intense personal religious experience, Christ showed me how much He loved me, and I discovered how much I loved Him. Truly I was overwhelmed.

The Appeal: Mere Christianity

No longer was I a liberal Protestant. I decided I needed a Church that was committed to "mere Christianity." (By this time, I had found C. S. Lewis, and it was like meeting an old friend. Was Lewis Orthodox at heart? Tell me about it!) I wasn't attracted by fundamentalism. I was somewhat drawn by the deep dedication and spirituality of Roman Catholicism in those pre-Vatican II days, but was put off by what seemed unwarranted additions to the Faith. I nearly became Lutheran but drew back because so much emphasis was placed on one man and one era; I wanted the common faith of the Church. Despite the warm spot from the wedding, I never looked seriously at Orthodoxy; it seemed so foreign and ethnic. What won my heart and mind was Anglicanism.

I went to Anglicanism seeking the Church. In the early 1960's one could argue that Anglicanism (though in British fashion it tolerated many eccentricities) was grounded in "mere Christianity." In those days even a "Low Church" Archbishop of Canterbury could proclaim, "We have no faith of our own. We possess only the Catholic Faith of the Catholic Church, enshrined in the Catholic creed." I was convinced. I was confirmed in an Anglo-Catholic parish whose ceremonies frightened me at first (was this idolatry?) but whose depth of liturgical piety and teaching soon captured me. God was present in the worship.

I remember visiting a Russian Orthodox parish about this time and thinking how much I had changed. Were it not for the ethnic nature of Orthodoxy, I thought I could fit in quite easily. I came across a book by one Professor Hodges which argued that Anglicanism was called to become the Orthodoxy of the West. I was delighted with the idea. With that vision in mind, I was sent off to the Episcopal Church's General Theological Seminary in New York City.

While there, an Episcopal priest told me, "No one loves the Episcopal Church. We're all in love with our image of the Episcopal Church as we would like it to be." I could see this among my seminary classmates: some were evangelical, some Anglo-Catholic, some liberal, and all these existed in many and varied permutations. If in Protestantism every man is his own Pope, in Anglicanism every man is his own Martin Luther, reformer of the Church.

Nevertheless, in the mid 1960's, the teaching at "the General" was still generally sound, and I managed to ignore such heterodoxy as existed. I already had my image of Anglicanism as

Western Orthodoxy, and in those days many others held the same ideal. I set out to shape my first parish in that direction and had some success. I was happy. I convinced myself and many of my people that Anglicanism at heart was really Catholic, really Orthodox.

I was wrong.

Bishop Robert Terwilliger of Dallas (recently departed, may God rest his soul) used to say that "Anglicanism is not a Church; it's a series of movements." Every couple of generations, Anglicanism shifts its ground. If I had understood that better, I wouldn't have been so shocked when, as time went on, leaders of the Episcopal Church increasingly began to encourage things which weren't "mere Christianity" at all: unscriptural doctrines, social action with no theological basis, women's ordination, abortion, sexual immorality—and finally, a reworking of the whole nature of God and the Christian Faith.

I had come into the Episcopal Church just as the latest Anglo-Catholic movement was winding down. For years I tried to convince myself it wasn't happening. Then I worked to restore "true" Anglicanism: I was active in national church affairs and was editor of *The Evangelical Catholic,* a traditionalist newsletter. But by autumn 1985, when the Episcopal Church elected a very liberal new Presiding Bishop and took yet another lurch to the left, I knew we had failed. The Episcopal Church was no longer my Church. I now look back at Anglicanism with profound gratitude but equally with profound sadness. I still believe Anglicanism was called to become Orthodox; she rejected her vocation.

Investigating Orthodoxy

During all these years, I continued warm toward Orthodoxy

from afar. I read Orthodox books: where else could one find sound theology and spirituality during the 1970's and 1980's? I took comfort in the presence of nearby Orthodox parishes and occasionally dropped in quietly. In the late 1970's, as times got tough in the Episcopal Church, I remember telling myself that, though my vocation was to be an Anglican priest, someday I would retire and die Orthodox. Why didn't I investigate Orthodoxy seriously during these troubled years? Partly because I was so dedicated to reforming Anglicanism. Partly because I assumed Orthodoxy was still so ethnic that it was inaccessible to those not born into it.

Now the hand of God entered in, in a very obvious way. In the summer of 1985, just before I lost faith in Anglicanism, my parish sent me off on sabbatical. When I left, I was a demoralized but still loyal Anglican. With no ulterior motives, I spent three weeks with the Orthodox Church in Greece and, for the first time, saw Orthodoxy close up. I was fascinated but perplexed. Orthodoxy didn't fit into any of my Western denominational molds. I had expected a rather remote, authoritarian sort of non-Papal Catholicism, but instead Orthodoxy appeared to be a dynamic, non-authoritarian, popular faith.

Greek Orthodox worship broke almost every liturgical rule I had long taken for granted—and yet it seemed to work; it was alive, and I couldn't understand why. At the conference I attended with other Americans, I found myself regularly taking the Orthodox position, even against other Anglicans. When the time came to go back to Anglicanism, I felt somehow as if I were leaving the Church. It shocked me. I decided I had simply been away from home too long. It was in fact the prevenient grace of God. By the time I finally lost faith in Anglicanism and began to ask, "Where shall I go?", God had already given the answer.

AN ANGLICAN–ORTHODOX PILGRIMAGE

I began to read Orthodox books avidly but found the mind-set hard to grasp. Suddenly, in December, 1985, while reading *Church, World, Mission* by Alexander Schmemann, my mind turned a corner. I saw the Orthodox Church as the true Church, united in Apostolic Faith, united at the Eucharist, and I knew that I had to be Orthodox—not "someday," but soon.

I still decided to move cautiously, afraid that I was just going through mid-life crisis. I was even more afraid Orthodoxy would prove to be a failure for me just like Anglicanism. Furthermore, my wife, Dianna, a deeply committed and believing Christian woman who had worked with me and supported me in our efforts to reform Anglicanism, was genuinely burned out. She had loved and lost and was afraid to love again. I believe when God wants a husband and wife to make a major move, He will inspire both of them to embrace it enthusiastically. So I decided to make no move until Dianna became enthusiastic about Orthodoxy. I would wait for God to take the lead and open the doors.

I made contacts with Orthodox clergy. Most were positive. I attended Orthodox worship and found it difficult for a long time. For the first time I realized how many converts Orthodoxy has: the "Russian" priest and cantor at the local Orthodox Church in America (OCA) parish were both of German Catholic origin!

Meanwhile, my parish knew I was in turmoil. Should I tell them about Orthodoxy? The answer came when, with an OCA clergy group, I visited the weeping icon of the Mother of God at Saint Nicholas Albanian Church, Chicago. After thirty minutes standing in awe of the icon, I had my vocation and knew what to do: I went back and told my congregation that I thought all traditional Anglicans ought to go home to Orthodoxy. I think they didn't take me seriously at first. I know my Episcopal bishop did not, or he would have intervened sooner than he did!

For two years, I taught Orthodox doctrine and also moved my parish towards Byzantine rite, on the principle that people need to *experience* something of Orthodoxy, not just hear about it. As pastor I felt called to proceed on this path as far as we could go and see what would happen. I offered them Orthodoxy. Some were enthusiastic; some were interested; some were patient; some were not.

Mutual Understanding

My wife and another woman from our parish attended Orthodox catechism classes at the OCA parish in the summer of 1988. Dianna said nothing of her reactions, and I was scared to ask. Then, one Sunday while visiting with old Episcopal friends, suddenly she told them all about the truth of Orthodoxy! I was flabbergasted and glad. God was opening the door to Orthodoxy for us together.

Now He began to move quickly. One evening before Evensong, as I stood before the Saint Nicholas icon I had brought back from Greece, I suddenly was given to understand that a new Saint Nicholas Church would soon be formed—one with which I was to be intimately involved. Such a possibility had not before occurred to me. I wanted to attend the Antiochian Missions and Evangelism Conference but felt I couldn't afford it—till a parishioner who did not know I wanted to go gave me a check which just covered the cost, saying she had been praying and had to do this. I attended and immediately knew where I belonged in the confusing American jurisdictional scene.

In the fall of 1988, my vestry unexpectedly pushed me about my intentions, and I told them again. The result was that (perhaps mostly to humor me) we invited a series of speakers in to help us determine our future together: a liberal Episcopal bishop (our own), a conservative Episcopal bishop, and Fr. Peter Gillquist from the Antiochian Department of Missions and Evangelism. At the end, I announced that I still believed Orthodoxy was the answer. Shortly thereafter, my bishop offered me the choice of resignation or an ecclesiastical trial—on grounds of "apostasy"! Dianna and I decided this was the final sign from God. I resigned.

And I was frightened. When I left the Episcopal Church in June, 1989, I knew of only five others who wanted to become Orthodox with me. I was prepared to take secular work. But God was merciful. Before we were done, about twenty-five people from my Episcopal parish joined us. Others, including a number of native Orthodox, joined as well. We were chrismated in September, 1989, and I was ordained.

God has since given us a beautiful multi-ethnic congregation which is a joy. I have never known such peace, such love. I have been supported full time from the beginning. By 1991 we had purchased two acres of property and had broken ground. We had twenty-five families, and we received our name: Saint Nicholas Church.

God and Saint Nicholas had it all planned from the beginning!

Orthodoxy is what I sought and loved for 30 years, long before I even knew it. In His mercy, God has finally brought me home. I hope He will give me many years to serve Him gratefully in His Holy Church.

Ancient Faith Publishing hopes you have enjoyed and benefited from this book. The proceeds from the sales of our books only partially cover the costs of operating our nonprofit ministry—which includes both the work of **Ancient Faith Publishing** and the work of **Ancient Faith Radio.** Your financial support makes it possible to continue this ministry both in print and online. Donations are tax-deductible and can be made at **www.ancientfaith.com.**

To request a catalog of other publications,
please call us at (800) 967-7377 or (219) 728-2216
or log onto our website: **store.ancientfaith.com**

 **ANCIENT FAITH RADIO**

Bringing you Orthodox Christian music, readings,
prayers, teaching, and podcasts 24 hours a day since 2004 at
www.ancientfaith.com

CPSIA information can be obtained
at www.ICGtesting.com
Printed in the USA
BVHW030850040620
580597BV00002B/181